Policeman's C

Harry Cole was [...] Bermondsey, Sou[...] when he was fourteen, during the war, and became a cricket-bat maker, soldier, stone-mason and, in 1952, a policeman. For thirty years, until his retirement in 1983, he served at the same police station in London.

He is a qualified FA coach (he has run numerous junior football teams), a referee and a keen cricketer. For many years he had a regular column in the *Warren*, the police magazine. His other books are *Policeman's Progress* (1980), *Policeman's Lot* (1981), *Policeman's Patch* (1982), *Policeman's Patrol* (1983), *Policeman's Prelude* (1984), *Policeman's Story* (1985), *Policeman's Travels* (1990), his two-volume autobiography, and *The Blue Apprentices* (1986).

In 1978 Harry Cole was awarded the British Empire Medal for voluntary work. Since leaving the force, in addition to writing he has taken up after-dinner speaking.

Harry Cole
Policeman's Gazette

Drawings by Graham Thompson

Happy Birthday!

All my love
Em 94.

Fontana
An Imprint of HarperCollinsPublishers

Fontana
An Imprint of HarperCollins*Publishers*
77–85 Fulham Palace Road,
Hammersmith, London W6 8JB

A Fontana Original 1992
9 8 7 6 5

Copyright © Harry Cole 1987

The Author asserts the moral right to
be identified as the author of this work

ISBN 0 00 637009 8

Set in Times

Printed in Great Britain by
HarperCollinsManufacturing Glasgow

Contents

To Daniel,
who makes me laugh

Preface

A few years ago, whilst breakfasting in my old South London police station (Carter Street, in the Walworth Road), I heard my umpteenth constabulary anecdote of the week.

'It's a great shame we don't record these tales,' commented Chief Superintendent John Allain. I instinctively looked around for somewhere to hide, for I knew what was coming. 'And I think you're just the man for the job.'

As a result of that conversation, I started a monthly station newspaper with the sole function of collating these stories. It operated under the rather grandiose title of *The Carter Street Herald Tribune*. Or as a former friend said, 'A ridiculous name for ridiculous tales.' This publication proved so popular (well, it was free) that I decided to widen my scope. A resultant appeal brought in anecdotes from such diverse spots as Oregon, USA, and Cwmbran New Town. The appeal was aimed mainly at the lower ranks; it is they, after all, who are usually at the sharp end. Interestingly enough, these stories are told frequently against the storytellers themselves. I am not sure what a psychoanalyst would make of that, except to confirm my theory that being a member of the police force is, quite simply, the funniest occupation in the world.

I therefore take this opportunity to thank all who helped and contributed to this collection, even those who changed their names, and for the fun they gave me simply listening to their tales.

Harry Cole
1987

The War and Before

From ex-PC Charlie Moxton
Between 1933 and 1937 I was posted to royal duties and part of my function was to patrol the grounds of St. James's Palace. There was a direct-line telephone from the local police station and it was customary for whoever was on duty in the station to notify the patrolling constable of anything out of the ordinary.

At that time the Prince of Wales had a habit of wandering around the grounds in the early hours of the morning and it was usual for the patrolling PC to be briefly, if unofficially, informed. My old friend Bert Standing, who was the night-duty telephonist, discovered that the Prince was on another of his nocturnal strolls and decided to phone me. I heard the bell ringing and made my way quickly towards it. I arrived just in time to see a figure replace the receiver, saluted him stiffly and snapped out a sharp 'Good morning, sir.'

'Are you Charlie?' he asked unexpectedly.

'Er, yes I am, sir,' I faltered, astonished that the Prince of Wales should know my name.

'Good,' he whispered. Then, putting a finger lightly to his lips, he glanced furtively all around. 'That was Bert on the phone and his message is: "Watch out, Charlie – he's about!"'

* * *

For a spell during the 1939-45 war, ex-Inspector John Telford was a sergeant at Paddington Green police station. During one particularly heavy German air-raid on nearby Paddington railway station, a bomb was heard whistling down. Experience had by then taught everyone it was going to be close. There was a universal dive for the floor and the reinforcing timbers shook dangerously as the bomb exploded just yards away.

One by one heads were raised and great sighs of relief could be heard as people realised they were still alive. Suddenly the outside door opened and an old copper entered. He was covered in dust and debris and, judging from the direction whence he had come, must have had a perilously close escape. In an obvious attempt to ease tension by throwing some light relief around, the inspector turned to the newcomer and asked him in mock severity just what he thought he was doing.

'Well,' said the bomb-blasted copper, 'I *was* going for a shit ... but I needn't bother now.'

* * *

Turkeys have become a recognised meal at most working-class Christmas dinners. Yet it was not always so. Many families could not afford a chicken, never mind a turkey – and if a turkey was expensive, what price a *goose*, for heaven's sake! One would have to be a millionaire ... or would one? Not according to ex-Sergeant John Coxhead, one wouldn't.

It was just after midnight on the day before Christmas Eve, 1938, when PC Arthur Trolley presented himself at the connecting door between the front office and the charge-room. 'Unlawful possession and assault on police, Sarge,' he announced. Now there was nothing stuffy or high minded about Arthur, and although he was sometimes a little quick to take offence, if he arrested someone then it was usually a bang-to-rights job. When I entered the charge-room there, sitting on the bench, was a small sad-eyed individual, who, although not quite drunk, had obviously allowed his patience to become impaired by drink. On the desk alongside him was a very naked goose.

Arthur gave an account of events in his best witness-box style. He said that he was patrolling his beat in New Cross Road, when he saw the prisoner hurrying towards Deptford with the goose across his shoulders. Arthur stepped out to question the man about his possession of the said goose, when the same man had thrown a vicious punch to the head of the constable and then promptly bashed him with the dead bird.

At the same time he made observations about police ancestry in general and his own present indifference to poultry in particular. Once recovered, the constable had cautioned the prisoner and marched both him and his goose into the station.

I invited the prisoner to offer his account of proceedings. To my surprise, he agreed word for word with everything Arthur had said. He then went on to say he was very sorry and hoped that he had not hurt Arthur's feelings in any way whatever. It had been, it appeared, a rather unfortunate chain of events, with Arthur's arrival being the last straw. He explained he had been to a Christmas club shareout at an Old Kent Road pub. During the course of the evening he won the goose in the public house raffle. It seemed a particularly apt moment to celebrate – so he did. Missing the last tram home. Eventually, somewhat unsteady on his feet and balancing the now wrapped goose on his shoulders, he set out for home. He had travelled barely a hundred yards when the first policeman appeared. What did he have in the parcel? the constable wanted to know.

'A goose,' he replied.

'Let's have a look at it then,' responded the suspicious copper, who might well have never seen a goose in his life. The bird was unwrapped, explanations both made and accepted and the little man resumed his lawful way home. Or rather, that was his intention but five minutes later another policeman appeared and asked to see inside his parcel. Yet again the wrapping was undone and explanations accepted.

Ten minutes later, at New Cross Gate, he was stopped by two policemen in a car. It was then that he decided it was a waste of time wrapping and unwrapping the bird. This was regardless of the fact that if a parcel on the shoulder excited suspicion, then a plucked goose around the neck would be of even greater concern. It was of course the cold naked goose bouncing across those narrow shoulders that had first interested Arthur. How was he to know that he was the fifth copper in thirty minutes who had expressed a desire to examine the creature? 'Very well,' the prisoner had thought. 'If you want it, mate, then you can bloody well have it,' and with that he had proceeded to batter the astonished copper with the twenty-pound bird.

It was at this point that raucous laughter broke out from the eavesdroppers at the charge-room doorway. It wrecked the usual serious atmosphere in which proceedings were conducted. Even Arthur's rugged countenance eventually cracked into a grin.

Handshakes all round, a quick cup of tea and a van ride home enabled our little prize-winner at least to finish his journey in style. Although what his wife made of his story, I dread to think!

* * *

From ex-PC 'Chesty' Sadler
In 1937 I was on duty in Oxford Street for the coronation of George the Sixth and Queen Elizabeth. It was a little after six in the morning and the dozing crowd had begun to stir. Of course there were no such things as sleeping-bags then, just blankets, coats and above all, newspapers. They were in a happy frame of mind as the last lap of their long wait opened up before them.

Suddenly a very cheeky busker somehow slipped through the police cordon and began to stroll down the centre of Oxford Street whilst strumming an old banjo. The tune he played, 'Pennies from Heaven', was a particularly popular one of the time. The result was astonishing. Thousands of pennies literally rained down from the crowd. He must have picked up a fortune!

Interestingly enough, not one copper moved him on – I think they were too busy marking where the pennies went!

* * *

Police Orders 24th July, 1860. *'Dismissal: PC 304 Hollis. Found asleep in a water-closet whilst under the influence of drink.'*

* * *

Police boxes were a vital part of the police force for almost half a century. Built of reinforced concrete, with small, iron-framed windows, the overall floor space was barely a yard square. They were little more than concrete cupboards, with a direct telephone line into the nearest

14

police station. Certainly up until the late 1940s men would be expected to take their meal-break in them and were frequently required to book off duty from them. The fact that the officer might still have to return several miles to the station *after* he had booked off was of little consequence.

Chris Stark, of the pre-war Kent constabulary, tells of one wartime night duty that terminated in a police box in very peculiar circumstances. It was at a few minutes to six o'clock that Chris had arrived at the box to enter up the written log, prior to handling over to his early-turn counterpart. At first, he thought his relief may be late but a banging on the door put these fears to rest and Chris threw open the door and prepared to dash away on his bicycle. To his surprise, he was not greeted by a blue-uniformed colleague but by a brown-coated cow, which immediately attempted to enter the box. Slamming the door, Chris hastily telephoned the station, where he was given very short shrift. 'Don't talk to me about bloody cows,' snapped the station officer. 'They're everywhere! They've escaped from the slaughterhouse and they're roaming about all over town.'

'Er, well,' faltered the perplexed constable, 'what am I supposed to do with it? I mean, I don't know anything about cows.'

'Good God, man!' exploded the station officer. 'Use your loaf! Put the thing somewhere safe for the time being. That's not a lot to ask, surely!' With that the receiver was slammed down.

This advice was all very well, but at six in the morning, in the centre of Gravesend, where can one possibly keep a cow 'somewhere safe'? Especially if (a) one's knowledge of cows is nil and (b) one hoped to be off duty within five minutes.

Chris gingerly opened the door and prayed that the animal had gone. It hadn't. Nervously easing his way past, he patted it gently on the rump and, for good measure, whispered 'Good boy' in its ear. The fact that it was referred to as the wrong sex seemed not to bother the cow in the slightest. For the want of any further inspiration, Chris tugged a tuft of grass from the nearby park and thrust it into the creature's face. The cow began to show an interest and moved forward inquisitively.

In the faint light of a pale dawn, the policeman was suddenly aware of the park bandstand. Of course! 'Find a safe place', the sergeant had said. Well, there's nowhere much safer, or less populated, than a November morning bandstand. He knew that if he could only entice it up the steps, then the bandstand could be the perfect place for a renegade cow. In fact with plenty of space and railings all around it could be the ideal place for the entire herd.

With a little pulling and a whole lot of pushing, the animal was finally secured in the municipal bandstand. Hurling in a few handfuls of grass for good behaviour, the breathless copper raced back to the box, where he found that his relief had just arrived. After officially signing the 'hand-over', Chris leaped onto his bicycle and prepared to race home to bed. Once a safe distance from the open door of the box, he called a parting message over his shoulder. 'By the way, Steve ... there's a cow in the bandstand!' He still claims he never understood even half of the adjectives hurled after him.

It was another two miles before he fully realised just how lucky he had been. This awareness was brought home to him when he saw another of his night-duty colleagues shepherding a bad-tempered and resentful cow along the road with his cape. This officer's humour was not improved by the fleeting advice from the speeding cyclist: 'Hey, Torro! Stick it in the bandstand!'

* * *

Police Orders 14th July, 1860. *'Pensioned off: PC Pryor "R" Division. Worn out.'*

* * *

From Cyril Green
The astonishing diversity of today's digital watches is very impressive but it's by no means a new thing. Take Frank, who was a detective constable at West End central police station during the early part of the last war, for instance. He had been given a birthday present of a very nice pocket-watch which could be set to give an alarm.

I was passing the CID interview room a day or so later, when I noticed the light was on. There was a table in the centre of the room and Frank was sitting on one side of it and a middle-aged women, very red in the face, sat on the other. Frank's watch was lying between them in the centre of the table.

Later in the day I asked Frank what it was all about and why the watch. He told me he had been interrogating the woman, who was suspected of theft, and had found her to be an enormous liar. He had therefore introduced her to his 'lie detector'. He told her that from then on, if she told him another lie, the bell in the watch would ring. The woman was so convinced by the 'lie detector' that she promptly admitted everything.

Until the novelty wore off, that watch was to crack dozens of the most difficult cases.

* * *

Police Orders 18th July, 1862. *'Reprimand: PC 192 Hawkins "S" division. To live in the section house ... and send the woman away.'*

* * *

From John Telford

The traffic in Hammersmith Broadway could clog itself up in minutes in the early thirties and it took three pointsmen to keep it on the move. There was Bridge Road, King Street and the Centre, all working in unison.

One morning I was posted to the centre point and the man at Bridge Road had released the traffic and sent it though to me. It was in the midst of this traffic that I saw the 'totter' from Notting Hill. He was sitting high on his pony and cart displaying rotten teeth, an unshaven jaw and a general all-round tattiness. As the horse trotted past, he leaned back into his pile of junk and hooked out an old lavatory seat. Placing it nonchalantly around his neck he gave me the broadest of black-toothed smiles and called, 'Fifty nicker for a Rembrandt, guv!'

* * *

From ex-PC Frederick Cumner

In 1938 I was stationed at Leman Street and, because of some shortage or other, I was seconded for a few nights to the Isle of Dogs. Whilst on patrol during that first night, I discovered it was impossible to get lost because there was only one road and that almost circuited the entire 'island'. On the second night I was approached by a colleague, who asked, 'Did you manage to stay sober last night?'

'Of course,' I replied. 'Why d'you ask?'

He then explained that it was the custom of local landlords to leave a couple of pints of bitter out on a ground-floor window-ledge for the night-duty copper. I thought this was a great idea and, although it was by then drizzling heavily, I set off in the rain well protected with my cape and leggings. Having discovered two pints at the first pub I came to, I decided to share my good fortune with my colleague on a neighbouring beat, who did not have access to such hospitality. Unfortunately, the sergeant chose that time to arrive on his nightly round of supervision.

'All correct, Sarge,' I reported dutifully as I tried desperately to keep the two pints from slurping from beneath the hem of my cape. We seemed to walk for ages before the sergeant finally said, 'Well, I'll be leaving you here.' He had moved away about five or six paces when he stopped as if struck by a sudden thought, 'Oh, by the way,' he said matter-of-factly. 'You can finish your pint now.'

* * *

From ex-PC Frederick Cumner

It was during my spell at Leman Street that we covered many tedious traffic points. One day I went to relieve Ginger Harrison, the pointsman at the bottom of Tower Bridge approach, for a smoke break. From this point one could see into the grounds of the Tower of London through a tunnel under the roadway. At night the tunnel was closed by two massive oak gates but remained open throughout daylight hours. 'Incidentally,' said Ginger, as he peeled off his traffic gauntlets, 'I did a valiant deed this morning. I stopped a runaway horse.'

'Good for you!' I enthused. 'What happened?'

'Well, it was the milkman's horse,' he explained. 'It was belting straight towards me with milk bottles bouncing about all over the place and the milkman in a blind panic running along behind. The trouble was that one half of that gate was shut.'

'So what did you do?'

'I shut the other bloody half, double quick!' said Ginger defiantly.

* * *

Police Orders 23rd April, 1860. *'Dismissal, PC 386 Kiddey "V" division. Being in a place of low resort.'*

* * *

Mollie Hill was a brand-new WPC at Vine Street in the thirties. On one of her first afternoons out on her own she was patrolling Piccadilly when she came face to face with a Chelsea Pensioner.

Face to face may not necessarily be the most accurate description of the meeting, because the rolling gait and rolling eyes indicated that the old gentleman had just left the local hostelry and he couldn't face to face anything for more than a split second.

She searched her memory for instructions for dealing with drunks in the streets. 'Arrest them and send for transport', was the recommended action. It was whilst she stood wondering that the taxi pulled up.

'What's up, luv?' called the driver. 'You look puzzled. New, are yer?'

Mollie nodded in agreement. She was indeed new and she certainly was puzzled.

'Don't worry, gel, stick him in the back. I'll take him home.'

'But I doubt if he has any money,' the girl pointed out.

'We don't worry about such things with these fellas, miss. All you've got ter do is forgit you've seen him – right?'

'Right!' agreed the girl, having just had her first lesson in discretion.

* * *

Police Orders 20th January, 1863. *'Rewards: Superintendent Gibbs, twenty-one pounds. PCs 181 Symes and 222 White, one shilling and threepence each.'*

* * *

From ex-Sergeant John Coxhead
The men on the beat are more likely to be seen patrolling in motorcars than on foot these days; Henry Ford and William Morris have something to answer for. The motorcar has changed everything. When I was first turned loose on the 'Z' Division public sixty years ago the superintendent had changed his pony and trap, only a few short years previously, for an open-body Bean motorcar. The sub-division inspector was still doing his rounds in a Chater Lea motorcycle and sidecar, complete with driver. The Flying Squad had just been initiated. It operated from Scotland Yard with a few cars – Lea Francis and Invictas with open bodies. The hoods were always up because they housed the wireless aerials, and the morse code operator sat in the back. Wheeled transport in nearly all stations was limited to the 'hand-barrow', so called because its proportions were similar to a costermonger's barrow. It did, however, sport a hood for such occasions as the removal of a corpse.

I remember one Saturday afternoon being sent with the barrow to bring in 'Old Kate', a local drunk. Our route back to the station was through the main shopping street. Kate, a born entertainer, was thoroughly enjoying herself; she was resting on one elbow as she lay on the barrow, just like Cleopatra, singing and waving to the cheering shoppers. What could I do but bear it with a somewhat sheepish grin? Anyway, some of the cheers were for me, I think.

When the station utility transport eventually arrived it was a Jowett open motorcar, powered by a 7hp two-cylinder engine. A sturdy little car but not very good at climbing hills in the Crystal Palace district. It was an improvement on the hand-barrow, anyway. I remember on one occasion having to send for the car to bring in Robert Euston. Robert was so named on being found abandoned on Euston railway station and taken to the local infirmary by a PC; he was accordingly registered in that name. He was a hard-working general labourer who did not believe in spending good drinking money on regular lodgings. Most of the time he slept in a tool shed on the local allotments. At court the following Monday Robert did not give his usual reply to the charge of drunk and incapable. ('I am very sorry. I do not remember anything. It will not happen again, Sir.') He seemed to think it noteworthy to announce that he had been 'arrested by the Flying Squad from Gipsy Hill police station'.

* * *

Police Orders 18th July, 1862. *'POLICE ATTACKED WITH DIA-RRHOEA. Superintendents to apply to the surgeon for the usual medicine.'*

* * *

From Claude Archer

After three years in Flanders during the First World War, I thought I had finished with mud. But soon after joining the force in 1919 I found a certain little old lady who had other ideas. 'Constable,' she said on a bright wintry afternoon, 'there is a poor little doggie stuck down there on the foreshore. I'm sure you can do something to help – can't you?' she added sweetly.

'I'll do my best, marm,' I replied, not realising just what I was letting myself in for.

Grosvenor Road runs between Chelsea and Vauxhall Bridges, and when the tide recedes the muddy foreshore is exposed some twelve feet below the level of the road. The only way down was by the Waterman steps. The 'sweet little doggie', of course, was marooned nowhere near the steps. Whichever approach I made there was going to be mud – yards and yards of it, thick, wet and evil smelling. As I approached, I began to sweet-talk the animal. 'Here boy! Here boy! Who's a lovely boy then? C'mon, c'mon boy.' 'Boy' was having none of it. Barking joyfully, he skipped and jumped into even deeper and smellier mud, much to the amusement of the small crowd that had begun to assemble on the embankment. Much advice was shouted as I splashed about in the mud. It was soon over my boot-tops, trouser-legs and even well up the tails of my old-fashioned 1919 overcoat. The further I went, the further went the wretched dog. My tour of duty was to have ended at 4pm and my relief had arrived but he was far too sensible to tackle the mud, although he did join in the general advice from above.

Eventually a friendly waterman in gum boots arrived and together we cornered and secured the mongrel. By this time the stench from the mud was overpowering and there was little to choose between either me or the dog. To make matters worse, the decomposed body of a cat had been disturbed by our frolicking and was giving off an odour all of its own.

Fortunately it had now become dark and, with my mongrel on a cord, I took the back-street route to my station, Gerald Road. In those days the charge-room on a Saturday evening would be like a madhouse, with scores of drunks arriving from Victoria and the surrounding area. Busy though he was, the station officer was not too busy to wheel around with an agonised expression on his face.

'What the hell – ?'

'Stray dog, sir. From the river-foreshore, sir,' I blurted, trying to justify my muddy state.

'Take yourself, that dog, and the bloody smell, and get out of here, boy – now! Hoppit and *don't come back*!!'

I tied the dog in the station kennels and set off home, with very peculiar glances from passers-by. Even there I had no sympathy.

'Where have you been?' said the wife. 'Your meal's burnt in the oven, I've been worried sick, and God, how you smell!!'

* * *

Police Orders 18th July, 1862. *'Dismissal: PC 466 Turner "N" Division. Drunk on duty, losing his truncheon and assaulting two civilians with his rattle.'*

From Leslie Triggs

It was 2am during the height of the London blitz and bombs had been falling for weeks. In spite of official statements to the contrary, morale, mine in particular, had definitely begun to wane. Suddenly a stick of bombs fell across the Woolwich Borough Council housing estate causing severe damage and casualties. I was on the scene within minutes and discovered appalling carnage. My first task was the obvious search for survivors. I approached the remains of one house that was little more than rubble – in fact, the only structure left standing was the staircase. Hearing faint cries for help, I pulled away the debris from the wooden door under the stairs. Inside I found an old couple, probably in their seventies. They were huddled together with their arms around each other and covered with dust.

Tragic and moving though the situation was, I suddenly found myself laughing. In addition to sheltering under the staircase, the pair had taken another precaution. Firmly tied on each head, and kept in place with a broad silk scarf, was a large saucepan! As I began to lead them away from the devastation, the husband asked, 'Where are you taking us, mate?'

'To the rest centre,' I replied. 'They'll look after you there and give you a nice cup of tea.'

'Hang on for a minute then,' he said, as he scuttled back into the wreckage. He soon returned triumphant and, with the words 'We've got to be properly dressed then,' he produced two sets of dentures, one of which he gave to his wife. There were other people still trapped so I pointed them in the direction of the centre and asked if they would be all right.

'Yes, don't worry yourself, we'll be fine, mate,' he assured me. 'If the buggers couldn't finish me off in Flanders, they certainly ain't going to do it in Woolwich!'

As they toddled off together towards the rest centre, my morale took an instant and much-needed leap.

* * *

Police Orders 28th September, 1860. *'Dismissal: PC 119 Bell "N" Division. Found asleep between two prostitutes whilst on duty.'*

* * *

From Claude Archer

As a recruit at Gerald Road police station in 1919, I was told by the duty officer to get the prisoners ready for the prison van. This van called daily around 7.30 am and conveyed all overnight prisoners to the local magistrates' court.

'It's the bloke in the first cell who may give you a problem,' he said. 'Apparently he's taken all his clothes off and won't put them back on again. Hurry him up, will you? The van's waiting.'

I entered the cell and it was immediately obvious that this was to be no easy task. He was a large rounded man and every time I placed any article of his clothing anywhere near him, he snatched it and threw it across the cell. I soon conceded defeat and returned to the duty officer. 'Sorry, sir, but I'll need some help. It's going to take at least three people to dress him.'

The inspector gave a deep sigh. 'Right, grab another PC and we'll see what the three of us can do.'

A couple of minutes later the inspector, an older constable and myself entered the cell and the naked drunk began rushing about all over the place. Being the youngest, it was soon made clear to me that I was to be the one to tackle him. That was only the first problem. The second was trying to get his trousers on. It was like trying to catch a goldfish in a large tank of water. Eventually the four of us were on the floor with the prisoner screaming 'Murder! Help! Police!' at the top of his voice.

'We *are* the bloody police, you fool!' panted the inspector from somewhere beneath me.

At last the trousers seemed to be in position, or certainly as close as we were likely to get them, so I tightened the belt.

'You've got them on back-to-front, you silly arse!' snapped a muffled voice.

'Sorry sir, but it'll just have to do. We could never get them *off* and back on again,' I pointed out.

He agreed and we bundled the prisoner into the van. He subsequently appeared before the magistrates with his trousers back to front and was fined one and sixpence.

I never saw the prisoner again but for the rest of my service at Gerald Road I was always referred to as 'Young back-to-front'.

* * *

Police Orders 16th July, 1860. *'Suspended: PC 125 Hallett. Until his eye gets well and he makes arrangements to prevent the recurrence of such discreditable quarrelling with his wife.'*

* * *

The younger generation, like all young generations, I suppose, seem firmly convinced there was no such thing as sex until they invented it. The average young policeman and woman are no exception to this trait. It came as a surprise therefore to hear of John Howe's early recollection of night duty in 1925.

'I crept under this railway arch at dead of night for a quiet smoke,' said John. 'I'd been there for a minute or so when I heard footsteps. I thought, hallo, they can't be up to any good at this time of night, whoever they are, so I puts out me fag and listens carefully. I thought perhaps it was a devious villain.' John paused for a minute and shook his head slowly. 'But it weren't no devious villain, it was a big fat moustachioed inspector who was creeping in for a quiet cuddle with a lady police officer in full uniform. She was wearing her big lace-up boots, an overcoat and wide-brimmed pith helmet. I thought, well that's all right, she won't come to much harm – they couldn't get near each other!'

* * *

Police Orders 21st April, 1860. *'Complaints have been made to the commissioner of dangers to pedestrians caused by orange-peel on the pavement. Constables are to remove pieces whenever seen.'*

* * *

From ex-PC Alf Dunwoody

Bill Waterson was everybody's idea of an old-time copper. He was big, round, affable and bewhiskered. He also knew more ways of making a shilling than any other dozen people I knew.

Take Tower Bridge, for example. Part of our manor was adjacent to the bridge and on pleasant summer afternoons it would be quite common for groups of tourists to besiege a passing constable. Bill never minded this, in fact he quite enjoyed it and on occasions he used a trick which became extremely profitable over the years.

He would take up a position some distance from the bridge where the spans could be seen but not the surface of the river. It would also be close enough to hear the warning bell. This bell would denote the approach of a boat and therefore the raising of the bridge. If during the course of his chats he heard the bell, then Bill would cease his planned dialogue and ask, 'Incidentally, have any of you ever seen Tower Bridge actually being raised?' Of course no one had because the bridge is raised only infrequently. 'Well, a mate of mine is on duty there today,' Bill would say, 'and if it's a bit quiet he may be able to give you all a treat. I'm not promising anything, mind, but I'll give him a wave and we'll see what he can do.'

Taking out a large but none too clean pocket handkerchief, Bill would wave frantically in the direction of the control tower. There was usually a moment's delay and then, to roars of approval, up would go the bridge!

The murmur of approval would only be matched by the jingle of silver and another bunch of tourists would go home happy.

* * *

26

Police Orders 18th July, 1862. *'Dismissal: PC 154 Foss "P" Division. Drunk on duty and throwing his hat in the road.'*

* * *

From Geoffrey Taylor, former pre-war PC
In the summer of 1938, a traffic-patrol car in Stepney was fitted with an experimental loudspeaker. It was attached to the front bumper and, being small, was not easily noticed. This was in the days when the police would give advice on road safety to passing pedestrians. The car had no obvious 'police' sign and whenever the speaker was in use few people seemed to realise where the sound came from. In Stepney Green there was a small service road running alongside the main road with a few bushes where the car could be parked unnoticed. The crew meanwhile would have an excellent view of the Mile End Road.

On Sunday afternoons, it was the custom for a seller of baigels to walk slowly along the opposite pavement looking for likely customers. A whistle would then emit from the loudspeaker and the baigel seller would stop and turn very slowly as he tried to locate the customer. The basket of baigels on his head would be very weighty and need careful balancing. This whole movement therefore would take some time. Unable to spot the 'customer' he would slowly resume his walk along the pavement. A few seconds later there would be another whistle and the same laborious performance would be repeated. Every Sunday would be the same and no matter how many times he was 'whistled' at he would stop and go through the same procedure. Occasionally, by variation, he would actually stop *between* whistles. We assumed this was in an attempt to finally discover the phantom baigel buyer.

After a few months the experiment was discontinued. Whether this decision made any difference to road safety is debatable – but it certainly made baigel selling a whole lot easier.

* * *

From ex-Insp. John Coxhead

Wartime saw many changes hoisted onto the force, not the least being the duration period for training. Many recruits would find themselves patrolling a beat within just three or four weeks of joining. Mistakes were therefore frequent. Take the wartime recruit who arrested a drunk on Christmas Eve, for example.

There were two main reasons for not arresting anyone for drunkenness at Christmas. Firstly, it was after all the season of goodwill. Secondly – and far more importantly – there were no courts held on Christmas Day. This meant that whoever made the arrest would be required to attend court on Boxing Day. Of course, if one is on duty on Boxing Day, then attending court is no great hardship. But usually a policeman will work only one of the two holidays. This means for any arrest made Christmas Day, or even late Christmas Eve, part of the Boxing Day holiday would need to be spent at court. This would not be popular with the constable, or indeed his family.

To be fair to war-reserve PC Bob Frost, he did try to avoid arresting the drunk. The only criticism was that he did not try hard enough. A flaw that no experienced copper could ever be accused of! It was about 1am Christmas morning when the PC stood at the charge-room desk and announced he had brought in a drunk and incapable. In anguished tones he explained that it had been unavoidable. A member of the public had not only complained about the prisoner but had insisted on accompanying the constable to the actual doorway where the prisoner lay.

When in funds, 'Blinder' Churchill's usual place of abode was the local lodging house. When out of funds – always through drink – it would be the deepest darkest doorway he could find. Blinder sat on the charge-room floor and listened to the constable's recitation with grand indifference. 'I'm sorry. Sarge,' apologised the constable, 'but I had no choice.'

'Well,' replied the station officer philosophically, 'as long as you're prepared to spend all Boxing morning at court, I don't suppose it matters.'

'All Boxing morn— but I'm day off, Sarge!'

'Unlucky, mate. You're the one who's nicked him ... so you're the one who's at court.'

'Isn't there anything I can do, Sarge?' wailed the recruit.

The sergeant thoughtfully gathered up some papers. 'It'll take me about five minutes to sort these out in the other room. Of course if I then come back and there's no trace of the prisoner, well' – he gave an exaggerated shrug – 'then officially he has never existed ...'

The best laid plans of sergeant and constable, however, failed to take into account Blinder's deliberate intention of spending Christmas in a warm dry police station, with all meals provided. Bob Frost had managed to lead Blinder out into the street without too much trouble but when the old reprobate realised what was happening he demanded to be rearrested. 'I know my rights, let me in!' he yelled as he banged continuously on the now closed front door.

'You'll have to let him in,' the station officer finally conceded. 'We'll have the neighbours complaining.'

Plan A had failed miserably. It was then time for Plan B.

A few minutes later, Blinder sat on a bench in the charge-room. Meanwhile, the sergeant, in an unusually loud voice, telephoned all the local police stations in order to discover one with a vacant cell. 'What's that you say? You've got one? Oh good! Just a minute.' He clasped his palm over the handset and addressed the recruit in an even louder voice. 'They have an empty cell at Southwark police station, Blinder. I'll get the van driver to take you both there. They also have an all-night canteen so you'll be better off in every respect.' He then removed his hand and spoke once more into the dead telephone. 'Yes, all night, thank you very much. The prisoner's on his way.'

Blinder's new spirit of cooperation was amazing as he trundled out into the night.

It was thirty minutes later that Bob Frost reappeared to report that Blinder was now safely, if not happily, ensconced for Christmas in the casual ward of the local doss-house. He had, it appeared, been rather abusive when, after assuring him he was in Southwark police station, the two coppers had suddenly legged it back to the police van. Blinder's anger was particularly understandable. As a person who was familiar with his 'rights' he was only too aware that the management of the institution also had 'rights'. These required that all beneficiaries must have a bath on admission – as well as doing a few chores before leaving in the morning!

* * *

Police Orders 24th July, 1833. *'Dismissals: PC Joseph Backwell and PC Joseph Bearhill "P" Division. Creating a disturbance outside the Star public house at 2am. Backwell playing a fiddle and Bearhill a tambourine to a great number of prostitutes who were dancing and making a noise.'*

Recruits

One great problem for present-day police recruits is the sheer volume of knowledge of everyday routine procedures that need to be learnt. In addition, everything seems to be known by initials, from VDUs onward. It is rather unusual for a recruit to find himself handling the control side of a station but of course it *can* happen – and a daunting experience it is too.

Take young Geoffrey Raines who, for an hour, was pushed into the role of station communications officer whilst that particular constable was having a meal break. He was asked by a panda car crew for a VDU check on a suspect vehicle.

'I'm afraid I'm not too sure how it works,' said the worried Geoffrey.

'Okay, don't bother using the VDU,' called the panda driver. 'Give 'em a ring on the phone – ask for CTB.'

CTB was as foreign to Geoffrey as VDU but he did his best. After many faltering explanations, he managed to contact CTB. The female operator there was of course fearfully efficient. This gave Geoffrey an even bigger feeling of inferiority.

'So, what is it you want?' she demanded.

'Er, a vehicle check please,' stammered the young man.

'Who is that?'

'Well, er, it's the police.'

'I know it is, you fool! But who?' (Meaning of course which branch of the force.)

'Well …' bleated the recruit, now very close to tears. 'It's me … Geoffrey.'

* * *

Tough as the East End of London can be for a copper, it does have its rewards. One of Dan Butson's favourite characters was a voluptuous

33

black lady who was passionately fond of young policemen. Just a little bit too fond in the case of one recruit, though ...

One of our loveliest characters, says Dan, was a lady by the name of Pearl Cohen. She was coal-black and almost six feet tall. She had a figure (when I first knew her) like Venus and just prior to the war had been a dancer in several West End shows. She had at some time married a Jewish gentleman but the marriage had gone wrong. This caused her to develop a dislike of everything Jewish. Whenever she became drunk (which was often) she would go around to the houses in the Jewish quarter and call them all the names she could lay her tongue to – and she knew a few!

It was usually at this time we would be called to deal with her. Which, nine times out of ten, would mean a drunk and disorderly charge. It would be at this stage that the fun would start, for as soon as she was arrested, a good-sized crowd would immediately assemble and all would be ready to offer advice on the best place to take hold of her. Or more to the point, where *not* to take hold of her. This would all be embarrassing for a young copper, to say the least.

Pearl, however, when she was sober, liked police very much and had often helped out some lone policeman in danger of being overwhelmed by local 'yobs'. On several occasions she had been known to wade in and flatten a few. One evening in Cable Street, her passion for young PCs unfortunately ran away with her.

I had turned the corner in company with a new recruit when we came face-to-face with the majestic Pearl. She was quite drunk and in a jovial mood. Giving one look at my colleague, she exclaimed, 'Oooh, he's lover-ly!' Without more ado she seized him tightly and began to smother his face in passionate kisses. In an effort to struggle free, he lost his balance and the pair fell to the pavement.

At this stage, I thought the experience would do him good and I stayed back to see how he would cope. Pearl, however, had deeper plans. Before he could recover from her overtures, she began to undo his trousers! Once more she was arrested for drunk and disorderly. Even Pearl wasn't allowed to go around undoing a constable's flies.

Sadly, though, the experience was all too much for the young man. Like a wronged virgin, he was never the same again and a week later he resigned.

* * *

All recruits need a little encouragement. So when the rosy-cheeked young Hove constable wheeled in a prisoner with the words 'I nicked him in the High Street, Sarge, after finding he's a disqualified driver', the sergeant said what any caring sergeant would be expected to say: 'Well, done, lad! That's a very good arrest. What have you done with his car?'

'Car, Sarge?' queried the puzzled recruit. 'He didn't have no car, Sarge – he was walking.'

Sadly, it is at times like this that sergeants drop their heads in their hands and murmur 'Oh f …!'

* * *

With the street disturbances of recent years, one tends to forget that parts of London have never been easy to police. John Howe recounts an early-turn parade just after he joined in 1925, that bears this out. The inspector entered the parade room clutching a bail enquiry.

'Who's on five beat?'

'I am, sir,' snapped John.

'D'you know where Marriot Street is, lad?'

'No, sir.'

'Well,' explained the inspector. 'Do you know Homerton High Street?'

'Yes, sir.'

'Do you know those two or three little alleyways down on the left?'

'Yes, sir.'

'Well, go down there then, lad, and when someone drops a piss-pot on your head – that's Marriot Street.'

* * *

35

Of course, it's not only rookies on the streets who suffer embarrassment … as the new female transfer to Scotland Yard's radio control unit will testify. A local citizen-band radio was playing merry hell with both transmission and reception. One garbled conversation was completely unintelligible except for the last two words which were 'four inches'.

'I'm sorry,' blurted the flustered young lady on the only clear reception for five minutes, 'but I'm only getting "four inches".'

'Well take off your shoes, darlin'!' came back the helpful reply.

* * *

For years now police officers have been convinced that all of society's interest seems to be for the criminal.

'It's only coppers who care for the victims,' they would claim.

Well anyone listening to PC Marco Hayden's commentary over his personal radio could be forgiven for believing that even that support has now vanished. After excitedly giving his location, Marco went breathlessly on to announce that he was 'Chasing … (pant … pant) … the … *victim*!' Each listening copper waited for the expected correction but again came Marco's transmission: 'Still … (pant … pant) … chasing *victim*!' By this time the 'victim' had doubtless decided that the world was against him and gave up. 'Victim … (pant … pant) … detained!' came the triumphant declaration.

'Unit chasing the victim,' cut in the station officer. 'I assume that the "*suspect*" is helping you?'

'… Er … (pant … pant) … Guess what, Sarge. I had it … the wrong … way … round.'

'I'll tell you what, Marco,' responded the sergeant wearily. 'Why don't you now run back to the station and let them both chase you?'

* * *

Alec Kirkpatrick was a large and likeable young Glaswegian. He had arrived at the station during the last week in April, a few days after the station football team had finished their season. Alec's summertime conversation consisted of little else but how he was looking forward to playing for the team the following season.

Training sessions began during the last week in July and Alec was always the first to arrive and the last to leave; he was an absolute fanatic. In addition, he was a more than useful player.

The first game was scheduled for the second week in September and it was to be a friendly against the local fire brigade. By the week of the match, Alec had worked himself up to a frenzy of excitement. Three days before the game, our secretary had rightly decided that our old black and white shirts were past their best and it was time for us to have an entirely new strip. This decision met with the approval of the whole team and we eagerly looked forward to our new attire.

It was the day of the match before we first saw the strip. As we each entered the dressing room we were given our shirt, shorts and socks. They were of a deep rich blue, with just the tiniest white trim. They looked so beautiful that everyone was delighted. Well, perhaps not quite *everyone*.

Alec Kirkpatrick was appalled. 'I canna play in *them*!' he exclaimed tearfully.

'Whyever not? They're gorgeous,' came the group reply.

'But they're ... they're ... BLUE!' blurted Alec, as if he had difficulty in just saying the word.

'Of course they're blue!' snapped the secretary irritably. 'Why shouldn't they be? They were the best in the shop and they cost us a bomb!'

'But ... blue ... is the colour of Glasgow Rangers! I'm a Catholic, I support Celtic. I can't *possibly* wear blue!'

'But you wear blue every day as a copper,' I pointed out.

'That's different. That's not *football*!' he remonstrated, as if I was a lunatic for confusing something as trivial as policing with something as serious as football. 'Besides, if I was to play *football* in a blue shirt, my father wouldna speak to me again.'

'Then don't tell him,' cut in the secretary logically. 'Just let it be our little secret. I'll tell you what, sunshine.' His anger was now rising.

'You'll either wear a blue shirt or you don't bloody play – it's as simple as that. Take your choice.'

Poor Jock looked like a rabbit with nowhere to run. He opened his mouth several times but not a word came forth.

'Why don't you play in two shirts if one upsets you so much?' asked the quiet voice of Don Vickers, our goalkeeper.

'What d'you mean, "two" shirts?' asked Alec as he desperately sought a loophole.

'Well, just wear another colour underneath and a blue one on top,' explained Don. 'That way you can honestly tell your old man that a blue shirt has not as much as touched your sensitive Celtic skin.'

'Ye...es,' said Jock thoughtfully. 'But the one underneath would have to be green ... if I was wearing a blue one on top, that is.'

'Oh, this is bloody ridiculous!' snorted the secretary. 'First you won't play in blue and now it's got to be green! Anyway green's a rotten colour for football shirts – it's unlucky as well!'

'Look,' persisted Don. 'I've got a tracksuit top in my bag. It's green of sorts, I suppose.' He rummaged for a moment then held it up. I would have agreed it certainly wasn't blue – but it was never green, not in a million years, it wasn't. If anything, it looked like a decomposing leper's cloak. It had obviously been put away damp in a plastic bag at the end of the previous season and was being confronted by air and daylight for the first time since. It did not look good. It also smelt evil.

To everyone's complete astonishment Jock's face lit up. 'That's great, mon!' he exclaimed. Before anyone could speak, he had slipped the fermenting garment over his head. 'I wouldn't touch that thing with the commissioner's dick,' opined an anonymous voice from the corner. But Alec was not to be put off. The fact that there was also a late summer heatwave and he would be playing in two shirts, one of them particularly heavy, seemed to matter not at all.

For the next few seasons, Alec was a regular in the side. The leper cloak had long been cast away and the good Catholic blood of the young Scot was warmed by a brave green and white striped Celtic shirt. I would have forgotten the incident, except that a few months ago I saw Alec for the first time for more than twenty years. He was by then a chief superintendent and in charge of security for the state visit of a foreign president. He was full of dignity and importance and in his smart blue uniform looked every inch the part. As I stared at him, he looked up and saw me. I wasn't sure if he recognised me (I've put on a few pounds since

38

then) or even if he wanted to. He suddenly mounted a horse and joined the royal procession. As he rode off down The Mall, I couldn't help thinking of that station football of a generation previous. 'I'll tell you what,' I said to the PC standing next to me, 'I bet that bloody poser's wearing a shitty green tracksuit under that uniform. Because if he isn't, his old dad will kill him!'

* * *

Senior sergeant briefing four probationary constables on their first day at the station: 'We all like to specialise in something. I prefer prostitutes. I find they are something you can really get your teeth into.'

* * *

New recruit to perplexed storeman: 'The inside of my helmet fits just fine, but the outside doesn't.'

* * *

Sergeant Ken Williams from Berwick showed a recruit the ritual involved in dealing with a dead body. Apart from being sick at his first sight of the female corpse, the recruit seemed to understand most of what was required. That is until he came to fill in a report book.

'She didn't make a statement, did she, Sarge?' he asked thoughtfully.

* * *

One of the greatest difficulties for any police recruit – some, in fact, find it insurmountable – is adjusting to the irregular hours of night duty. Take Bert Ransden for example. By two o'clock in the morning, Bert's eyelids would have started to droop. By three o'clock he would be colliding with stationary objects such as lampposts and sandbins. By three-thirty, if he had not 'got his head down somewhere' he would be almost delirious. It would be at times like these that the exquisite pleasure of a road-mender's hut would be most appreciated. That pile of old sacking lying by a roaring coke brazier would have the sheer luxury of a four-poster bed.

These cosy roadside havens are, of course, few and far between. More often than not, the punch-drunk recruit would have to make do with a derelict car, or, if he was lucky, a shop doorway. Of course some shop doorways are better than others, some are, in fact, quite desirable. Take Robinson's the newsagent's, for instance. This doorway was not only deep but it also had a heavy wooden gate across its entrance. This gate was never locked and, by slipping a hand through the bars, could easily be unfastened from the inside. Once through the gate, the old police greatcoat could be spread out in a corner and an uninterrupted sleep enjoyed. Then, about four o'clock, the first of the early-morning office cleaners assembling at the nearby bus stop would arouse the slumberer with their girlish chatter.

During Bert's first few nights in the force he found himself in an awful dilemma. Firstly, he was awaiting the adventure that he had been assured was around every corner. But secondly, he knew that even if it was there, he could never stay awake long enough to recognise it. This was probably best illustrated on the night he was 'brutally assaulted'.

He had staggered back to the station with a bloodied and busted nose and the makings of two enormous black eyes. Our first impressions were that he had been hit by a truck or ambushed by robbers. In fact it was nothing so sinister and only a recruit would have even admitted the cause of the injuries.

Bert had apparently been doing his nightly impression of a dormouse, when the drama had taken place. It was the roar of the engine and the dramatic screech of brakes that first roused him. Emerging from his slumbers he was immediately aware of running footsteps. 'It's a smash-and-grab!' he thought. After all, the TV shop was only next door. Lifting his head from the warm sanctuary of the greatcoat, he was briefly aware of a faint rustling noise immediately above him. Before he could focus his eyes they were closed for him by an almighty wallop straight in the centre of the face. The blow knocked him straight back to the coat and left him dazed and groggy. Their deed apparently done, he then heard the footsteps race back to the vehicle, and, with a crashing of gears, the engine noise faded into the darkness.

Who, or what, had been his assailant that could deal him such a demoralising blow and disappear into the night before he could assemble his wits?

Perhaps it was still there?

Bert groped for his torch and, as he illuminated the doorway, he found the cause of his injuries lying on its side, impassive and bloodstained. He had, he discovered, been brutally attacked by a half-ream of *Daily Mirror*s that had been heaved over the gate by the delivery man. That was distressing enough, but the noise of another approaching motor told him that he had just thirty seconds before he was attacked by *The Times* and *Sporting Life*.

'I suppose,' said Bert ruefully as he gingerly bathed his nose, 'it's why it's called a hard-hitting newspaper.'

* * *

New Hackney recruit on his first use of the personal radio: 'Could I have a vehicle registration check, please?'

VDU operator: 'Yes, go ahead with the number.'

Recruit: 'EYK 443C.'

VDU operator: 'Well done, this is a stolen vehicle. Is it driveable?'

Recruit: 'Er, I'm afraid I really don't know ... I've only got the number plate.'

A few days later the same recruit came up on the radio once again. 'VDU check, please.'

VDU operator: 'Can I take it you actually have a vehicle this time?'

Recruit: 'Yes.'

VDU operator: 'Very well, go ahead with the number.'

Recruit (after a long pause): 'Well, there's no number on it. The plates have been removed.'

VDU operator: 'Is there any number at all you can give me?'

An even longer pause, then thoughtfully: 'Will a tyre number do?'

* * *

Like many other such occupations, the force does have a tradition of 'setting up' or 'winding up' many of its recruits. Some are obviously more gullible than others. For police sergeant Dick Andrews, the recruit he had at Catford a year or two ago was a 'winder-upper's' dream.

The young man rejoiced in the nickname of 'Mushroom'. 'This,' explained Dick, 'was because he had been kept in the dark and fed on bullshit.'

The shift was late-turn duty (2pm–10pm) and Dick had been required to attend a distant court that particular afternoon. He was therefore not in his customary role as sergeant when the relief paraded for duty at 1.45pm. In this situation, the senior PC will usually deputise and allocate the men to their beats and duties for the day. Unable to resist such an opportunity, the 'acting sergeant' had given Mushroom the Metropolitan Police wind-up chestnut, of the 'water sample test'. This test was to be carried out at a former boating pool that Sainsbury's, the multiple store, had just purchased and planned to turn into an ornamental lake. This act required the cooperation of several other people. There was the teleprinter operator, for example, who would be needed to tap out an official-looking message; forms were needed, plus of course the sample bottle. Last but by no means least, was the Metropolitan Water Board who, by now, must be as familiar with nutty coppers as they are with burst drains. In addition to the sample, Mushroom was told a sketch-plan would be required of everything in and around the lake.

'Everything?' asked the puzzled lad.

'Everything!' he was instructed. 'If it's there, sketch it! We don't want a disease breaking out just because you're too bloody idle to draw a sketch.'

Sure enough, a few minutes later, Mushroom trooped out of the station clutching his bottle, wellington boots, forms and sketch sheets.

It was later that afternoon that Dick returned from court, knowing nothing of the dreaded water-test. At 10pm, as the late turn filed in to book off-duty, Dick asked the eternal sergeant's question at dismissal time: 'Any reports?' Two fights and an accident were handed to him but these were routine. It was Mushroom with his reams of paper that really caught his attention. 'What's this then, Mushroom?'

'The water-test, Sarge. I've taken the samples to the water board, they said to thank you very much.'

It did not require a genius to realise what had happened. Dick went along smoothly with the joke. However, he felt he should at least say something further to the young man. 'Er, no problems, were there?'

'Well, only with the sketch plan, Sarge. That was particularly difficult.'

'Why was that?'

'Well, it was the ducks, Sarge ... they kept moving!'

* * *

From ex-Sergeant Dan Butson

The Christmas of 1947 was my first year in the force. It was also a time of great shortages that were, in many ways, worse than anything we had experienced during the war.

Together with an older PC, I was working a dual traffic point at a junction just in front of an off-licence. Because of the intense cold (it was a bitter winter) the owner of the shop had promised to allow us to buy a half-bottle of Scotch once the point had finished. This was particularly good of him because whisky was extremely difficult to obtain in those days. I did not drink whisky at the time and I had arranged to give mine to my older companion who really enjoyed it. As I came out of the shop, I slipped on the ice and fell flat on my back with the scotch in my hip pocket. The old PC suddenly ran panic-stricken through the traffic and, instead of helping me to my feet, rolled me roughly over onto my side and felt frantically for the bottle. 'Thank God!' he exclaimed, his eyes closing in reverent gratitude. 'Oh thank God ... It's not broken!'

* * *

A frightfully well-spoken, genteel middle-class lad named Dudley arrived at Carter Street police station in South London to begin his police career. This is an area that is as removed from well-spoken, middle-class gentility as it is possible to get. During his first day out, he was called to an accident that involved a car with rather strange number plates. Dudley queried this with the communications office via his personal radio.

'They've never been issued,' said the communications PC.

'What does that mean?' asked the confused Dudley.

'It means the car is probably a ringer,' he was told.

'I see,' said Dudley, who in fact didn't 'see' at all. 'So what should I do now?'

'Check the number on the tax disc.'

'That number is also different,' observed Dudley a minute or so later.

'Then nick him,' came the curt advice.

'I beg your pardon?'

'Nick him!' repeated the communications man. 'Swift him in, arrest him, call it what you like but get him in here double-quick – it's a bent car!'

'I couldn't possibly do that,' exclaimed the trusting Dudley. 'He's such a delightful chap!'

There is no doubt that Dudley did fetch an old world courtesy into the area. Take the stolen car chase, for example. Just before 5am one morning, two men were stopped in possession of a stolen car. Both sprinted off in opposite directions and one was soon captured. The other, it was discovered, was an escapee from prison, named Stanton. The area was thoroughly searched and a few minutes later Dudley came upon a shadowy figure lying under the back axle of a partially hidden Ford.

Kneeling down alongside the vehicle, Dudley bent forward and enquired apologetically, 'Excuse me, sir, is your name Stanton?'

* * *

One curse that modern-day police do not have to contend with is the dreaded 'number one dress'. This was a tortuous, Gilbert and Sullivan-type outfit that weighed a ton and was used on all ceremonial occasions. The trousers were of the heaviest serge and would all but stand up by themselves, and as for the tunic, belted with a wide leather strap at the waist, it was fastened so dangerously high that it could remove adenoids. Anyone required to wear it would have one instant ambition: to remove it as soon as possible. It was hot, heavy and uncomfortable.

It did have one little advantage, though. Whilst appearing to be pocket-less, two large pockets were in fact concealed in the twin tail-flaps at the rear. It was truly astonishing what little treats could be concealed in these flaps. The average duck's-arsed copper could therefore produce more surprises from the region of his buttocks than a whole host of magicians. As ex-PC Alan Marshall now relates . . .

PC George Cutler was a rotund, crafty, perpetually tired, amiable soul. He was not unlike Mr Wimpy of the Popeye cartoons. As a young and inexperienced constable, I must say I was impressed by his casual and unflappable approach to life in general and police duty in particular.

On the day of a grand state occasion, I was posted with George to a small enclosed square near the Houses of Parliament. Here there is a private access into the underground system for Members of the House. Once there, we were completely isolated from the public by a temporary wooden structure some twelve feet high. Our duties were to prevent sightseers from climbing the fence or using it as a vantage point. The entrance to this tiny underground station was in semi-darkness, caused by the shadows of the brilliant sunshine; it was a natural haven for two sweaty, number-one-clad constables.

We soon realised that our presence was totally unnecessary and, being out of sight, George immediately removed his tunic. This left him in a short-sleeved, cream-coloured vest, decoratively set off by wide red-and-white-striped braces. Laying out his cape on the floor, he sat down at the top of the steps with his helmet perched on the back of his head in lieu of a cushion. Taking the hint, I joined him. Once he had made himself completely comfortable, he rummaged around in his discarded tunic and promptly produced two bottles of beer! We were at peace with the world as, puffing out clouds of cigarette smoke, we twiddled our toes to the beat of the passing, but unseen brass band.

Suddenly, from the dark depths of the staircase, came the sound of metallic scraping – it was like a chained medieval ghost. A small uniformed figure emerged, with glazed, bespectacled eyes that blinked frantically at the unaccustomed sunlight. As the figure drew closer, our first impression was of a Japanese admiral, complete with oversized sword that dangled dangerously between his legs. His cockade hat was sideways and at an angle of forty-five degrees, as were his 'Harold Lloyd' spectacles. In an effort to avoid our feet, he tripped over his sword. Staggering on a pace, he finally collapsed onto the recumbent George. It was then that George astounded me. In the time it took the 'admiral' to disentangle himself from our legs, George had whisked away his bottle, removed the fag from this mouth, thrown up a quick salute and snapped out a quick 'All correct, sir!' to a rather unsteady commissioner of the Metropolitan Police! Hauling up the celebrated gentleman, whose hat was now firmly over his eyes, we reverently brushed him down and pointed him in the direction of the exit. He took a moment or two to get his bearings, then, muttering to himself, tottered off, dragging his sword behind him like the conducting rod of a tram.

I stared in amazement at the departing figure before turning to the still placid George. He had already resumed his relaxed position. He looked at me thoughtfully for a moment before restoring his crumpled cigarette to his pursed lips. 'Well son, after that ...' he paused as he puffed a great cloud of satisfying blue smoke, 'it'll be all downhill.'

* * *

From ex-PC 'Chesty' Morgan
It was shortly after midnight that I was patrolling the Holloway Road during the late spring of 1937. I had been out of training school for all of four weeks and I was still looking for that first 'big moment'. Suddenly there it was, or at least it could be: a small side door of the huge Gaumont cinema was ajar! I slid into the opening and followed the passageway through a labyrinth of twists and turns before emerging finally into the vast dark auditorium. Well perhaps not *completely* dark,

because there, across the two thousand-odd seats, were three small dancing torch lights and a motley of muffled but excited voices.

I extinguished my own lamp and crept slowly closer for a better view. To my utter astonishment, I discovered that I had not been the first to stumble on the open door; at least three of my colleagues had beaten me to it. Not only that, but at that moment they were trying various switches in order to raise the organ! A sudden cry of triumph from Taffy Lovell indicated success in this venture and slowly the great wurlitzer rose up from the orchestra pit.

'Give us a tune, Taff,' came the request from the darkness.

Taff did his best to oblige and, after a few false starts, he began to pick out a recognisable medley of Irish songs. I eased myself down onto an end-of-row seat and began to take stock. What sort of profession had I joined, I wondered, when at one in the morning, in a London cinema, I was listening to a trespassing Welsh policeman playing Irish songs on a German organ?

* * *

Coppers it seems have always been frustrated artistes. A generation later, across the other side of London, another half-dozen policemen found a door open ...

The old Trocadero cinema at the Elephant and Castle could seat thousands and was one of the largest of its kind in Europe. Sadly, during the cinema recession of the early sixties the mammoth 'Troc' was one of the first to close its doors.

It had been shut for barely a week when, at three in the morning, a sharp-eyed night-duty PC found one of its forty or so doors open. Because of its sheer size, seven or eight constables spent the best part of an hour searching the place – all to no avail. There was still a great deal of property there and even the electricity remained connected. Eventually, one or two of the searchers wearied of the chore and began to play 'silly buggers'. One stood on the edge of the stage and told a few 'I say! I say! I say!' jokes to the remainder, who had sat themselves in the front row. Once he had exhausted his repertoire, the fattest of the group then appeared from the wings with an old bicycle, which he proceeded to ride around the stage firstly with no hands and secondly, and very wobbly, with no feet. This act received great applause from his assembled colleagues.

So engrossed were the searchers, that they failed to realise that the duty officer, Inspector 'Jimmy' James, had discovered the same open door and was by then lost somewhere in the interior of the building. Following the sound of the hilarity, the inspector finally emerged at the back of the circle. On carefully opening a door, he could see there, on the stage, one of his more mature constables riding a bicycle with no hands, with yet another of his trusty men sitting on the handlebars. Before Jimmy could say a word, the bicycle gave one final great wobble and crashed into the huge draped curtain.

'*Oi!*' boomed Jimmy from the circle. 'What the bleedin' hell do you think you're playing at?'

'Sorry, guv,' said the burglar, rising up between the seats of the row in front, 'but I only came in for a kip in the warm.'

Unfortunately, the two sacks of lead fittings that lay alongside him told a different story but, as Jimmy was to point out later, 'It's my opinion he gave himself up before you lot formed a choir.'

'I Didn't Say I Was Silly'

From PC Colin Hobday

The dramatic finish of the Iranian embassy siege was seen worldwide on television screens, but for the days and nights preceding the assault it was excruciatingly boring. Coppers lurked everywhere but nothing happened. It was during the long silence of the early hours that the 'voice' was first heard.

Over the entire personal radio network came an anonymous muffled yawn followed by the deadpan announcement: 'I'm bored.'

Dozens of coppers mentally concurred but no other sound was heard. That was until some thirty minutes later, when the voice again yawned and announced this time that it was 'still bored'.

It was the third declaration of boredom that finally provoked the assistant commissioner into life. Seizing the personal radio of a nearby police inspector, he angrily cut in. 'Will the unit who keeps claiming he is bored identify himself? Over.'

There was silence for a moment, then the voice reappeared. 'I said I was *bored* – I didn't say I was *silly*!'

* * *

One of the functions of juvenile bureau officers is to liaise with schools. This necessitates talking to groups of all ages from the very young to the mid-teens. It was the latter age group that PC Derek Blake found himself faced with one afternoon. He had covered a fairly wide range of subjects during his talk and shortly before finishing asked if there were any questions. One nubile young black girl instantly raised her hand. 'I've been told I'm a nymphomaniac,' she announced casually. 'Can you tell me what it means?'

Now, wide though Derek's range may have been, it had not been *that*

51

wide. However, he manfully struggled to explain to a class of twenty girls in general and one girl in particular the precise definition of a nymphomaniac. While he was at it he also pointed out some disastrous repercussions that can lead from promiscuity. Having faltered his way through ten minutes of insatiabilty, degradation and venereal diseases, he asked the questioner if she understood his answer. 'Nah,' she said, 'cos you're definitely wrong there anyway.'

'Am I?' asked the surprised policeman. 'I think you'll find I'm not.'

'Well, I'm a nymphomaniac and I ought'a know,' reproached the girl. 'You can take it from me that a nymphomaniac is someone who can't help nicking fings.'

* * *

Two constables, who although really quite friendly always seemed to be arguing, were called to a sudden death in Camberwell. 'Y'know,' said the first as he looked down at the corpse, 'for a bloke of sixty-three he's in very good nick.'

'He's f … g dead, you idiot!' responded his friend despairingly.

* * *

From PC Jim Harding

A young PC was on duty outside the Spanish embassy when at 3am he called for help on his personal radio. A sergeant eventually arrived and discovered a rather eccentric gentleman giving the PC the benefit of his lifetime of experience, which, by then, he had been doing solidly for the previous two hours.

'I don't know how to get rid of him, Sarge,' said the PC almost tearfully. 'He's sending me barmy.'

'Don't worry, son, leave it to me.' The sergeant then turned his attention to the eccentric gentleman. 'Now then, sir, you must be perished. Wouldn't you like a cup of tea or something? I'm sure we would if we weren't compelled to stay here. Why don't you pop off and get one? There's a good chap.'

'You're quite right, Sergeant,' said the eccentric. 'Excellent advice.' He immediately hailed a passing cab and disappeared from sight. The sergeant then spent the next thirty minutes lecturing the young constable on how one needs to 'assess' the best way to handle people. 'All comes with experience,' he prattled smugly.

By this time the PC was beginning to regret the departure of his previous companion. Just as his eyes were glazing over, the taxi returned. Out stepped the eccentric gentleman, together with three deck-chairs, a small table, a silver tea-service and biscuits! 'You will join us, Sergeant, won't you?' he beamed generously.

* * *

A Camberwell constable, presumably attempting to introduce a brand-new system of breathalysing: 'Right sir, I will require you to inhale this bag with your breath.'

* * *

From John Bailey, retired PC from Egham
I was, for a period of my service, employed as an enquiry officer at Staines police station. The majority of this work entails the taking of statements from witnesses, victims and offenders, of various incidents. In such cases appointments have to be made days beforehand and a strict timetable adhered to.

One Saturday afternoon, I was riding the station light-weight motorcycle (known throughout the force as the 'Noddy') across to Feltham for such an appointment, when I noticed the policebox light flashing. On answering, I was told by the communications officer at Staines that 'Some clown has gone to Scotland for his wedding at four o'clock this afternoon but he has forgotten his certificate banns. Nip over to the registrar's office and see if anyone's in.' I made the short journey to the registrar's office only to discover it was closed.

In my next conversation with the communications officer, I acquainted him with this fact and asked him if he could ascertain if by any chance the registrar lived locally. The reply came back within minutes – we were in luck! The sought-after gentleman lived but half a mile away. Leaping on the Noddy, I breezed to the house only to discover that he was officiating at another wedding several miles away. He would, however, his elderly mother informed me, be home around 3.30pm. I decided to wait. Mounting the Noddy once more, I sat alongside the village green and just watched the world go by. Sure enough, exactly on cue, I saw the registrar approaching his home. As he pulled up I stopped alongside him and propped the Noddy on its stand. At first he looked extremely worried but I soon eased his mind and explained the circumstances to him. I accompanied him to his office where we both saw the relevant piece of paper. With just fifteen minutes to go there seemed little we could do about it but I telephoned Staines police station and asked if there was a number in Scotland we could contact. There was! The registrar quickly rang the number and spoke to an official, who promptly decided he could not accept such details over the telephone. 'For all I know,' said the cautious Scot, 'you may not even *be* the registrar.' As an afterthought he told us that if we could possibly get the certificate to him before eight o'clock he could marry the couple before the nine o'clock deadline. This of course left just one problem; how to get a certificate of banns five hundred miles in a little under four hours? Well one thing was sure, we couldn't post it. The registrar and I talked it over for a few minutes. The only people strictly entitled to the paper were both in Scotland, but a little fast talking on my part and I had the certificate.

Now there were no flashing lights or two-tone horns on the Noddy, just a flat-out speed of about fifty perilous miles per hour. I just had to keep my fingers crossed and ride as fast as possible to the police office at Heathrow airport. As I roared into Heathrow, with the old Noddy engine almost quivering with delirium, I fortunately spotted two police officers in a mini-bus. I quickly explained the position and asked if there was a British Airways shuttle to Edinburgh in the near future. There was – and we had five minutes!

I jumped aboard the mini-bus and it roared away with blue light flashing through the tunnel and the security access point, to the aircraft's side. The dispatcher, seeing a police vehicle, stopped and waited for us to run up the stairs. Once in the cockpit, I explained the position to the pilot, who agreed to take the certificate on condition he was met at the destination. I, of course, agreed and he was obviously delighted to be a part of what was quickly becoming a combined operation.

I eventually made my way back to Staines, where the duty officer wanted to know where the blazes I had been all afternoon. I made my explanation and he nodded an unofficial approval of my actions. He then proceeded to mark the 'result' space in the original message as 'Assistance rendered'. These two innocuous words happily disclosed nothing of my extremely unofficial toing and froing at Heathrow.

Making a quick call to the groom's house in Scotland, I then arranged for him to attend the airport to collect his precious certificate, with of course the essential assistance of the Edinburgh police. Almost as an afterthought, I asked for the identity of the person to whom I had been speaking. (This was for my own peace of mind; I didn't want to fail at the last hurdle.) I was appalled to discover it was the local newspaper reporter who was covering the wedding! Shit! I had been absent from my beat for the best part of three hours; I had done the grand tour of Heathrow airport; I had misused police petrol (heinous crime, this); made false statements; involved some half a dozen others in my scheme and in fact done almost everything except actually go to Scotland myself. If this local hack fancied offering a paragraph or two to the Sunday papers, I would certainly have some explaining to do. Well, if I was in for a penny then I was certainly in for a pound. There were therefore two other calls to be made. The first was to the Edinburgh airport police to ask them to complete the job I had so innocently started, and the other was to let the registrar know the saga we had bred.

The following day I fell upon every Sunday paper I could lay my hands on. I searched every inch of every column before breathing a sigh of relief – there was not a mention! This left almost a week before the local papers came out. I think I had lost pounds by Friday.

We were safe! Again not a mention!

On reflection, I think it must have been one of the best-kept secrets of all time. It was such a secret that the happy couple, who, incidentally, made the deadline with minutes to spare, must have believed the certificate was sent by the good fairies. That can be the only explanation, unless of course they found they really hated each other – because they never sent a word of thanks to anyone!

* * *

Sergeant Carl Rogers found a gas cylinder leaking in a South London street. The brigade had already been called when Carl decided that it might help to reduce the risk if he turned off the gas. Much to his astonishment, fire appliances arrived from all over South East London. These were further augmented by a few ambulances. Although all three services were then in position, no decision could be taken until a big white chief arrived from the fire brigade. It was around this stage of the proceedings that it was realised that the sergeant had actually turned the thing off. 'You're not allowed to do that!' he was told. 'A leaking gas cylinder is a full emergency.'

'Sorry,' said the apologetic Carl. 'Would it help if I switched it back on again?'

Fire engines then seemed to be full of firemen hiding their grins while their white-helmeted seniors tried to decide what should be done with a 'full emergency' that had been completely ruined by an interfering police sergeant.

* * *

It was a beautiful morning, one to warm the cockles of Gordon (Flash) Hampton's heart. He was posted early-turn panda car driver and his area covered Sundridge Park golf-course. For Gordon, this was akin to a drunk in a brewery. As a golf fanatic there was always one urgent priority for Flash – to get to the course as soon as possible. After all, anything could have happened during the night. It could have been stolen or something – stranger things have happened.

Well, he thought, as he drove into the driveway, the clubhouse is all right; perhaps I'd better just check the greens. It was this decision that was his undoing.

Gordon, you see, was not the first to arrive at Sundridge that morning, neither was he the second. 'Oi, Gordon!' called a familiar voice as the constable strolled towards the first fairway. Gordon turned in some surprise; he had not expected anyone so early. 'I think you'd better wander over there and have a look, Gordon lad. There's something you ought to see.' The newcomer pointed vaguely towards the centre of the course.

'Fiery Fred', as he was called, was a local character, quite well known on the course. Alcohol tended to affect his imagination and there was no doubt that in spite of the early hour, he was already brimming over with imagination fluid.

'What is it, Fred?'

'Well,' said Fred, shaking his head sadly, 'you're not going to believe it but –'

'Try me!'

'All right,' replied Fred with uncharacteristic assertion. 'There's a flying saucer on the first fairway. How about that for starters?' Gordon placed his hands on his hips and stared at the odd fellow in undisguised disbelief. 'I know what you're thinking,' continued Fred. 'You're thinking I'm pissed. Well maybe I am, but pissed or sober, that's still a flying saucer!'

Deciding there was nothing to be gained by any further conversation, Gordon moved off towards the fairway. The problem with flying saucers is that no one really knows what they look like. Or rather they don't know until they actually see one. Gordon now knows *exactly* what they look like. They are circular, silver in colour, four feet in diameter – and bleep. At least that is what the one in the centre of the first fairway did.

When one really comes to think about it, all manner of scientific questions are posed by a flying saucer on a suburban golf-course. Does it play golf, for instance? Gordon approached the thing and circled it nervously. He had no doubt what it was; it was unquestionably a flying saucer, although there appeared no means of entry. The obvious question was what to do about it.

As Gordon was to sensibly point out later, inspectors earn more money than constables. He therefore called one on his personal radio. Now this was all very well, but it did lead to the second question – namely how do you best tell someone you have just disovered a flying saucer?

'Let me get this straight, Hampton. You say you just discovered a flying saucer?'

'Yes, sir.'

'What are you doing at Sundridge Park, Hampton?' Duty officers, you see, always suspect the worst of their men. The whole incident would now become a personal thing between them. For the rest of his service the inspector would be convinced that if Flash had not been traipsing about all over a golf-course, then the flying saucer would never have landed there in the first place.

'Does it really *matter* what I'm doing, sir?' demanded the exasperated Flash into his radio. 'The point surely is that I'm here – and I've found a saucer!'

The sense of this remark was bravely pointed out to the inspector by Sergeant Richardson. 'After all, he is right, sir – and it doesn't happen every day, you know.'

'Very well, Sergeant,' growled the inspector vindictively. 'As you feel that way about it, perhaps you'd better come with me. Tell Hampton we'll be with him in about fifteen minutes.'

Flash spent those fifteen minutes crouched in a bunker, convinced that with the sort of luck he was having that day, the saucer would fly away before the inspector arrived. At long last the second police car nosed its way into the driveway and Flash was soon joined by his betters. The sergeant, it transpired, was something of an expert. 'It certainly looks like a saucer,' he said thoughtfully. 'But it's never come through space, that's for sure.'

'Why not, Sarge?'

'Seams,' he nodded wisely and pointed to the centre of the object. 'It's got seams. They would have busted in outer space.' He gingerly approached the rounded edge and held out an open-palmed hand in a rough temperature test. He slowly closed the gap before announcing, 'It's cold.'

'Right,' asserted the inspector. 'Put it in the back of your panda, Hampton. We'll take it back to the nick.'

'What?' protested Flash. 'It's still bleeping! Supposing it's radio-active or something?'

'You heard what Sergeant Robinson just said,' snapped the inspector. 'He said it was cold and he knows about these things. Besides, you're too old to have children. Now will you stop messing about and shove it in the back of your panda!'

Flash eased the police car as close to the fairway as he dared. If it should ever come to a test as to what really frightened him, it would be no contest at all – the green-keeper would win every time. The three brave scientists then humped the thing into the back of the panda and Flash bleeped away towards Bromley police station. Some twenty minutes later, still bleeping merrily away, the saucer was dumped on the table of the station charge-room. In situations like this 'experts' will come out of the woodwork. There will be at least one CID officer who 'knows about these things'. There will also be an old soldier who, if not watched carefully, will attack it with a hammer. And there will also be a rosy-cheeked recruit who has seen every science-fiction film of the last eight years and knows all the right expressions. Finally however, there will be the 'reserve man'. The reserve man is the man (or woman) who is in charge of the station communications room. If anything is going on anywhere on the manor, then he or she is supposed to know. This time he was to excel himself. He entered clutching a piece of paper.

'Did you find this on the golf-course, guv?' he asked thoughtfully.

'Certainly did,' agreed the inspector officiously, already having visions of at last the Queen's police medal. 'And I have fetched it in to protect the public.' Flash, it seemed, had already been rowed out.

'Well, if I was you, guv,' whispered the reserve confidentially, 'I'd take it right back again.'

'Whatever for?'

'It seems that half a dozen apprentices from Farnborough aircraft workshops have spread 'em all over the South of England. It's a jolly jape apparently. Not bad either – eh?'

'It's a what?!' yelled the inspector, wheeling round. 'Hampton! Where's Hampton?' Flash, however, was nowhere to be found, though the noise of the panda's engine could be heard fading into the distance. Towards the golf-course, perhaps?

* * *

Distraught victim at scene of burglary: 'They even took the bidet off the bed!'

* * *

Two years after the last war, there were still great shortages of both luxuries and essentials. However, many of the beaches had been cleared of mines and at least the traditional charabanc outing to the seaside had returned.

It was one of these ancient vehicles that had caught recruit Dan Butson's eye. It was standing apparently empty in an East London side street with the driver at the wheel and its side lights on. As Dan approached, the driver gave him a quick shrug and pointed over his shoulder to something outside the coach.

Still new and eager, Dan was aware of a continuous noise and strode boldly around to the side of the coach where he grandly flourished his torch. The beam of his lamp had illuminated the bums of thirty-five cockney charladies, each crouched over the kerb with their knickers around their ankles!

* * *

Lady tourist to PC Alan Wood who is standing on the Victoria underground line, on Victoria station, beneath a sign that reads VICTORIA: 'I'm trying to get to Marble Arch, Officer. Can you help me?'

Knowledgeable PC Wood: 'Certainly, madam. You need to get a train to Victoria, madam, and change there.'

* * *

Bill Morton was known at the station as the 'Mobile Pig'. Not so much for his features but for his habit of frying bacon every day for his meal break. It was the general opinion that should he ever wind up on a mortuary slab, then the word *'Danish'* would be stamped right through him.

One night, around 4am, when one's resistance to cold always seems to weaken and a general exhaustion and chill sets in, Bill was patrolling his beat in a dark unlit warehouse area. After a while, he was gradually aware of a rise in temperature. Moving closer to a wall, he found it pleasantly warm and he supposed there was a boiler or somesuch on the opposite side. Like manna from heaven, he let the sheer luxury of the unexpected glow envelop his whole body. Pressing his back to the wall, he felt his joints revel in the sudden thaw. This sudden feeling of comfort and well-being, also prompted a desire for sleep. Leaning back, he parted his legs, dropped his chin to his chest and fell into an instant and blissful cat-nap ...

He awoke with a start and the beam of a powerful white searchlight blinded his eyes. He now recalls that his immediate reaction was one of terror, like a trapped bomber over enemy territory. (He found this equally puzzling, having spent his entire war-service in the Navy.) Struggling free of the glare, he found that blue lights were flashing and a fire tender escape ladder was extended high above his head. The warehouse was ablaze!

The approaching fireman asked him if he was okay and to Bill's utter astonishment added, 'And what a lovely smell of roast pork! It's a bleedin' bacon factory!'

* * *

There are times when, in an effort to be professionally detached, policemen become insufferably pompous. Take the young mental patient who made four unsuccessful attempts to throw himself under trains. Each attempt was only thwarted by the superhuman efforts of the Dog-Kennel Hill station staff. In his report of the incident, the even younger policeman wrote: 'The patient appeared agitated.'

* * *

A particularly horrific murder took place in South London in which a tramp was cut up with an electric carving knife and his dismembered body scattered in various rubbish bins and dust chutes throughout the area. PC Ian Hill was one of the many officers who were required to search in likely places for any remains.

Being drawn to one bin by a particularly offensive smell, Ian soon uncovered a large piece of decomposing flesh. Unpleasant though the task was, the constable considered it was at least a good job well done.

Or at least he *did* until the pathologist pointed out the words *'New Zealand'* along one side.

* * *

From ex-Sergeant Dan Butson

One dark November evening just after the war, I was strolling along my beat in Wapping when I saw three or four young boys, none of them older than twelve, pushing a wheelbarrow with a 'Penny-for-the-Guy' sign laid across the chest of the dummy. I was some yards past the group before I had second thoughts. There had been something about the face that struck me as being unusual. It appeared to be very real and yet, at the same time, unreal. It certainly looked like a face but at the same time it was unlike any face that I had ever seen before.

'Here, hang on a minute!' I called back. 'What's that on your barrow?'

They looked apprehensively at each other, before the oldest brazened it out with a chirpy reply. 'It's a "Guy", ennit?'

'Where'd you get it from?' I persisted.

There were more furtive glances and again the assurance that 'It's a Guy ... honest, mister!' – a sure sign of something amiss.

I pulled back the old sacking that covered the torso and discovered that the 'Guy' in question in fact had a sporting chance of being the *original* 'Guy'. These charming lads had discovered a way into the bomb-damaged vaults of the local church. They had also found that several of the old lead coffins had split open. With a sharp eye for a penny, these little entrepeneurs had been trundling a centuries-old mummified corpse up and down Wapping High Street for the best part of two hours!

With the assistance of the vicar, I returned the body to the coffin, only to discover the following day that they had had it out twice more that evening.

At first there was a certain revulsion amongst the local congregation but, as the curate was later to point out, the old chap probably had more rides two hundred years after his death than he ever did whilst he was alive!

* * *

PC Mick Wharton did an inquiry to an address and stated that he did not think the family in question lived there.

'There are four families shown on the doorbells,' explained Mick, 'and they're all named Friedland.'

* * *

It was very obvious that PC Archie McCormack's prisoner really *had* been drinking. 'His speech was slurred, Sergeant,' recited Archie, 'his breath smelt strongly of drink – and his eyes were *diluted*.'

* * *

From ex-Sergeant Ron Fernell

A few years ago I was stationed at Romford as a sergeant and received the usual warning to parade at midday for a special operation. This was obviously going to be a bit different from the usual 'Black Gay Whales Against the Bomb' demo, for no one could tell me what our assignment was to be. Rumours circulated, the most favoured being a drugs raid on Hendon Training School. At twelve o'clock, seven of us climbed aboard a minibus and set off for an unknown destination.

At this point I should describe one of the PCs who figures prominently in the happenings. PC Bell, or 'Dinger' as he was better known, weighed in around twenty stone and this was distributed in generous lumpy proportions around his 6ft. 1in. frame.

We made our way along the North Circular and eventually joined many similar vehicles in the Hendon training school. Sergeants and inspectors were ushered into a large briefing room and there we were told that if we expected to see our nearest and dearest before the following morning we were sadly mistaken. Our assignment was to last long after that but if we wished to phone home we could do so. Once our calls were made the switchboard would close, so secret was our mission.

Our task for the coming twenty-four hours was then revealed. We were to be part of a raid on every major gaming house in London. The success of the operation depended on all the clubs being raided at the same time, ie 2am. In order to prevent the doormen operating any warning bell it would be essential to gain entry as soon as possible. In our case it would be up six steps and straight through the front door, a task for which Dinger had obviously been created.

At 1.53 am came the signal. Our minibus swung into the turning and we were outside the club. Dinger, having wound himself up, sprang from the coach and hurled himself towards the steps. On reaching them, he immediately fell over. Hitting the ground like a chimney stack, he lay on his back with his legs in the air. The rest of our splendidly rehearsed team either tripped over him or cracked up laughing. With surprise now gone for a Burton I feared the worst, but when I looked up into the entrance, the doormen were also in a state of collapse.

Righting Dinger, we followed him through the door and were amazed to find that still the doormen had been unable to raise the alarm. With the raid being such a success, all the credit went to Dinger. He was obviously a weapon of such sophistication that even the most villainous club could not hope to compete.

* * *

From a Stoke Newington husband-and-wife dispute
Husband: 'Hit her? Of course I hit her! I'm entitled to hit her. All she ever does is nag. She never stops!'

Wife: 'I should think I'm entitled to bleedin' nag! He spent all last Saturday afternoon at the hypermarket and all he bought was two pair of everlasting socks. I wouldn't even mind that – but he's had them on a week!'

* * *

We have come far from the traditional East London pubs of yesteryear to the trendy wine bars of today. This is never better illustrated than by Dan Butson's recollection of one dark evening in 1947 when he was taken short on his Leman Street beat.

'I popped into the gents at the rear of this pub,' writes Dan, 'and stood quietly in full uniform doing what was necessary. Suddenly, in came a young woman who bade me good evening and then proceeded to squat down alongside me and relieve herself of a few gins.

'I couldn't understand at the time why she didn't use the Ladies. But on recounting the story later to my colleagues at the nick, they said the pub was one of several in the area that made no provision for women. They had been built in the days when women did not enter public houses. Well, not *respectable* women anyway.

'It took me ages to get over it. Nothing like that had ever happened to me in my home county of Dorset!'

* * *

PC Nicholson could see just how badly the victim was upset and decided to at least try to reassure him with a smooth professional approach. 'And now, sir, what *exactly* has been taken as a result of this burglary?'

Tearful victim: 'Well, there were two early nineteenth-century French carriage-clocks, for starters. They were at the very least one hundred and fifty years old.'

The PC made careful note of the subsequent description. 'Okay sir, I've got all that. Were they the battery-operated type?'

* * *

From Sergeant Graham Batho
A young constable was assigned to assist at the entrance to the Royal Garden Party at Buckingham Palace. A long queue of dignitaries and

VIPs stretched away in the distance, including a full-blown Royal Navy admiral complete with sword and lady wife.

The lady wife soon began to show signs of irritation at the delay. After suitable prompting from her, the admiral approached the young policeman and asked the cause of the delay. Having answered umpteen similar questions that afternoon, the young man replied, 'Well, you see, they've run out of bread and the Queen's mum has nipped out for a loaf.' The lady wife was still not amused but the admiral almost fell over his sword as he asked, 'Are you sure you were never in the Navy, Officer?'

* * *

Extract from the statement of a victim of a motorcycle theft. 'I identified my motorbike. It was intact apart from the ignition switch, top box, indicator, silencer, crash-bars, brake-lever, twist grip, handle-grips, mudguard, rev. counter housing, headlamp rim, mirror, handle-bars and tool kit. All to the value of £400.'

* * *

Much time and money has been spent in recent years in attracting the graduate recruit into the force. The main problem with many of these youngsters is that their Latin is often greater than their commonsense. Take Neil Edwards's reminiscence of one young girl.

It was (surprise, surprise) in the early hours of the morning that the 'bomb' was first discovered. A biscuit tin with wires and a battery does look convincing, particularly to anyone who has never actually seen a bomb, and the well-spoken young police lady who attended soon pronounced it thus.

Following a quick message into her personal radio, a more worldly copper may have been a little suspicious of the prompt response that poured out of the set. It came in from all quarters. One or two colleagues actually attended, keeping, of course, a safe distance.

Now, it is all very well *finding* a wretched bomb but having found it what does one *do* with it? When in doubt take it back to the nick, seemed the general advice. Helpful though this was, the 'nick' was over two miles away and the biscuit tin was heavy. How about transport? There was a general intake of breath at this. Police transport regulations, she was informed, clearly prohibit the transportation of bombs. 'I would *like* to help you, really I would,' said one sympathetic driver. 'But if the thing was to explode I would probably get suspended.' He sighed helplessly. Suddenly his eyes lit up as a thought struck. 'There's the answer – over there!' he pointed to the darkened superstore across the road.

'Where?' asked the puzzled girl.

'There – that trolley. You can push the thing back to the nick on a supermarket trolley.'

'Won't that be dangerous?' queried the girl dubiously.

'Dangerous? Of course not!' said the driver scornfully. 'What we'll do is escort you front and back. That way there'll be no chance of any innocent party being blown up.'

Within a few minutes the procession was under way. With a flashing blue-lamped police car in front and another fetching up the rear, to say nothing of two pandas and three police vans trailing directly behind, the girl spent the next forty-five minutes trundling the 'bomb' on a Safeway trolley back to the station.

It was almost two minutes to booking-off time, before she was somewhat nervously told that the biscuit tin was in fact just that – a biscuit tin.

Her reaction to the 'bomb' may have been naive but her reaction to the 'biscuit tin' was anything but. In fact the station emptied quicker from her wrath than it would have from twenty pounds of gelignite!

'It didn't make any difference though,' says Neil, 'She's still as daft as ever.'

* * *

Of course, as Neil Edwards also points out, male graduate entries can be just as naive as their female counterparts. Take one particularly gormless individual who, at three in the morning, discovered an intriguing red button in the communications room. He found it so fascinating that he pressed it – and immediately set off the air-raid siren. Fortunately another officer was close enough to switch the thing off before the local population decided the Russians were at Tilbury. Now although our idiot had, in common with most people living on the manor, heard the siren, it was soon realised that he had no idea whence it came (the station roof).

'Send the prick out to look for it then,' growled the old station officer. 'If he's daft enough to set it off he can try to bloody well find it.'

'But it's up on the roof, Sarge,' pointed out the van driver.

'*I* know it is, you fool – but he doesn't know it! Send him up to that conglomeration of sports grounds at the top end of the manor. That should keep him out of the way for a while. Tell him the siren's on top of a pole or something and, if it's still whining, to let us know.'

'Sarge – it's pissing down out there!'

The station officer raised his eyes scornfully. 'He won't shrink! In any case, he's such an idiot, I doubt if he'll even notice.'

Five minutes later, suitably wrapped against the elements and in search of the siren-topped pole, the young graduate set off for the perimeter of the manor.

Twice in the next thirty minutes the searcher reported over the radio but, with a rather dramatic car chase taking place elsewhere on the ground, he soon became forgotten. It was nearly three hours later that he returned, freezing, to the station, covered in mud and soaked to the skin. 'I'm sorry, Sergeant,' he said apologetically. 'I looked everywhere but I could not find anything that looked remotely like a siren on a pole.'

'Never mind, lad,' said the station officer, feeling quite remorseful that the joke had gone this far. 'Get a nice hot cup of tea and slip away home and dry yourself out.'

'I really am sorry, Sergeant,' persisted the well-mannered youth. 'But neither of us could find it.'

'*Neither* of you?' queried the station officer.

'Yes, Sergeant. Neither me nor the groundsman.'

'What "groundsman", lad?'

'The one I woke up to help me look for the siren.'

* * *

Ten minutes after a bearded suspect committed an armed robbery in Westmoreland Road in South London, a young PC stopped a man who he thought could be the bandit. He immediately informed the station via his personal radio.

'Has he got a beard?' asked the communications man.

'Well ... no,' replied the young constable grudgingly. 'Look, I realise it's a long shot ... but he could have dashed home for a shave!'

* * *

A Reading burglar mistimed the opening hours of a block of offices and as a result found himself still on the premises as the staff arrived. Panicking, he hid under a large double-desk, where he remained for well over an hour before dashing for the door. The PC who was called interviewed the typist under whose desk the intruder had hidden. She was a large-thighed young damsel with a short leather skirt.

'Anything you can tell me about him, luv?' asked the PC hopefully.

'Nothing at all, really,' said the girl. 'The first I knew he was there was when my drawers went up and down.'

* * *

Female victim of car theft, on being asked if the car had reversing lamps: 'No, I use the mirrors.'

Bewildered PC: 'Well, what sort of tyres did the vehicle have?'

Lady Victim: 'Oh, unquestionably good ones.'

* * *

From Dennis Traher
Metropolitan Police General Orders state that any members of the force

may put forward suggestions to improve the efficiency of the force and, if adopted, their scheme may merit some reward.

An enterprising young sergeant policed an area that was exactly on the flight-path to Heathrow airport. There was also a particularly large reservoir nearby and he pointed out that should a plane make a forced landing, the police would be first to the scene. They would therefore need at the very least a boat to effect any sort of rescue. The scheme was considered by Management Services and it was decided to give the sergeant a chance to prove his theory. M.S. were not over-happy about the project but felt that after having it drawn to their attention, they couldn't very well ignore it ... just in case!

An inflatable dinghy and outboard motor, small enough to fit in the boot of a panda car, were supplied and the great day dawned – grey and wet. There was a large open-fronted boathouse on the shore and nearby bobbed some forty sailing-dinghies. Because of the rain, the assistant commissioner, his commander and a dozen or so other assorted senior observers assembled in the shelter of the boathouse. The Underwater Search Unit then placed two frogmen in the water to simulate survivors and everyone was ready for the off. For the purpose of the exercise, a small passenger aircraft was considered to be fictionally ditched in the centre of the reservoir. The panda car was the first to arrive. The sergeant (or mad inventor) alighted and with the help of two PCs carried a large box to the water's edge. The box was unfastened and the revealed dinghy then had to be assembled and inflated with two foot pumps. It was twenty minutes before the thing was launched. The larger of the two constables then hopped in and began to pull manfully towards the 'incident'. His second pull missed the water completely and he promptly fell back in the boat. This little setback caused one of the oars to float away, which was only recovered with some difficulty. The sergeant, meanwhile, had tried to start the engine with a rope and toggle. This task naturally required all of his attention and he therefore failed to notice that the overweight constable was now splashing merrily towards a moored yacht. The resulting collision caused him to fall forward into the dinghy from his kneeling position in the rear.

It was whilst he tried to resume his kneeling position that the engine fired. The boat took off like a punctured balloon. The two hapless frogmen, who were patiently treading water and waiting for a rescue, took instant fright and dived to avoid being struck by the rogue dinghy. The throttle then briefly stuck and for a minute or so the boat appeared demented. The note of the engine faded as the dinghy all but disappeared. However, a quick pivot turn caused it to race back once again towards the frogmen. Suddenly, and to everyone's surprise, the boat slowed and the 'survivors' were quite easily rescued – forty minutes after entering the water!

The common-sense verdict on the whole operation would have been to forget it. On the other hand Management Services had visions that immediately they did so some idiot would pancake a 747 straight into the deep end. A compromise was reached which equipped just one Panda with a rescue dinghy. And everyone agreed that, should the unthinkable happen, they all knew where they wished the inventor.

* * *

It is amazing in police work how many times the layman notices the little things that totally escape the experts. Take the police inspector who was trying to talk a man down from the roof of the institute of psychiatry, for instance.

'I've spoken to the doctor, guv'nor,' said PC Carl Thomas, 'and they say he's not mental.'

'I see,' said Inspector Lord thoughtfully. 'Perhaps you should ask them why, if he's not mental, he is sitting on a roof in the middle of the night eating a cider bottle?'

* * *

PC Douglas Cable was on duty at the Charlton v. Cardiff football match when he was told by an inspector to draw a personal radio from control and take up a position on Charlton railway station. It was further pointed out to him that although he would be on his own, if he should suspect trouble was imminent he was to radio for help immediately.

'You can't have a radio,' said the bloke at control. 'We don't have enough as it is.'

'Well, suppose there is any trouble?' asked the wary Douglas.

'Well, the station is five minutes' walk from control – but you'll find if there's any aggravation you can run it in fifteen seconds.'

* * *

From ex-Sergeant Dan Butson
One baking hot July day not long after the war I had to drive the 'non-descript van' containing the chief inspector and one male and one female sergeant, to a narrow street where they could keep observation on a brothel.

The non-descript van is usually an old battered vehicle that will look in character wherever it is parked. It will have slits for vision and a hole in the floor to pee out of – and not a lot more. Because of the heat, I had instructions to park the van in the shade of a tree close by the house we were watching. I was then to lock the doors and call back for it in a couple of hours. In the event of an emergency the occupants could gain an exit via the back door that only unlocked from the inside.

When the time came to return, to my surprise there was no sign of the vehicle. I did have a passing worry about this because I had the only set of keys to the thing. I called for assistance and, together with several other officers, began to search the area. We made the mistake of searching the *streets*, when in fact the van was quite close by on a bomb site. Apparently a fire had occurred and the brigade had been unable to squeeze past the van or unlock the doors to move it. They had therefore manhandled it onto the site and parked it in blazing sunshine with the rear doors flush against a wall!

The chief inspector had originally decided not to 'show out' in order to protect the observation but two hours in baking heat with no windows or doors had given him second thoughts. Not only that, but at least two of the three needed to use the hole in the floor. By this time of course the fire was out and the brigade had left. From their new position they couldn't even see the brothel any more. In fact all they could see was half a dozen damn fool coppers walking up and down the surrounding streets, looking for a van!

* * *

Sergeant Mick Summerby heard a call over the r/t that stated that a passing pedestrian had noticed that an occupant of a large flashy car was in possession of a pistol. The car had apparently been stationary at the traffic lights and the alert informant had caught a glimpse of the weapon as the suspect had moved his jacket.

The given location was just a few streets away and sure enough, moments later, the suspect car swung into sight. The police vehicle did a quick U-turn and within seconds the suspect was draped over the bonnet of the car with feet astride in the best Starsky and Hutch manner. A brief search soon revealed the gun.

Mick then turned his attention to the female passenger ... Princess Margaret.

* * *

PC Russ Hardingham to a driver he had just stopped: 'You have been drinking whilst having too much to drive.'

Russ's colleagues swear that the driver offered him the bag to blow in.

* * *

Rather inebriated witness to a Southampton nightclub assault: 'Anyway, I can't stand any of those bloody queers. To my mind they deserve all they get.'

Second witness: 'But he's not a queer, he's definitely heterosexual.'

First witness, indignantly: 'Well *they're* even worse! They go with horses!'

* * *

Keeping long observations on suspect premises can be a mind-blowing task, especially on cold winter nights. It does, however, have the occasional reward, as Tony Jauncey relates:

There had been several break-ins at a rather posh North London golf-club and six members of the local constabulary decided to give it a full night's coverage. They arranged to meet at the thirteenth hole to plan the observation. Four of them arrived punctually but they were still waiting for the last pair when running footsteps were heard. 'Come quick!' said the newcomer, who was one of the two missing consta-bles.'You really must see this!' His urgency caused them to join unquestioningly in the sprint to the edge of the course. 'How about that?' he asked triumphantly as he pointed to the rear of a large house that overlooked the course. Clearly illuminated was a tall incredibly statuesque blonde beauty. She would have been a stunning-looking girl at any time, but completely nude and massaging her ample curves with body lotion threw the best-laid plans of the constabulary into utter confusion.

As the five watched in silent worship, there was a sudden almighty crash. Could it be the phantom robber, taking unfair advantage of their distraction to perform another of his dastardly deeds? Thankfully no. It was just the missing sixth member of the group falling out of a nearby tree. The crash was also heard by the nude who, showing scant regard for both the English winter and the eyesight of six London coppers, promptly threw open the window. She then called out in the peculiar broken English that only German au-pairs will use: 'Who ist dis?'

'Er ... it's the ... er ... police, luv ... You see—'

'Der politz?' she cut in.

'Er, yes, Miss, the police.'

'Ach, der politz! Ah vell, ist okay den. Gooden nicht.'

So saying, she closed the window and resumed her massage.

* * *

It really is amazing how many times villains carry out well-planned and sophisticated crimes yet overlook the most basic essential. Take the silver Rolls Royce that was stopped by police in the King's Road, for instance. It had, it transpired, been stolen three months before and all the plates had been expertly changed.

In such cases one would assume they had been changed to that of another Rolls Royce – but no. When the police check was made, the reply came back: 'Well, it's not a Rolls Royce, mate ... what you should have there is a Reliance Moray Tug that tows aircraft off Luton airport's runway.'

* * *

Whenever a police officer reports an accident, he is expected to gather all relevant details. For this he will doubtless need witnesses. When PC Roy Squire attended at one accident, he couldn't believe his luck – there were three! 'Did any of you see what happened?' asked Roy hopefully.

'Yes, I did, sur,' said the first man in a thick Irish accent. 'I'm the bloke what called you.'

'Oh good,' exclaimed the delighted Roy. 'Now before we start, can I have your name and address please?'

'Yes, sur. My name is Donovan and I live at 64–'

The second witness (Irish too) cut in sharply, 'You can't live there, *I* do. *You* live at 62.'

The third witness (also Irish) then cut in equally sharp, 'No, no, no! *I* live at 62. *He* must live at 60.'

Roy then turned to the first witness and asked him (understandably) how long he had lived there – wherever *there* was.

'I'm not sure,' said the man, screwing up his face thoughtfully. 'I think it's five years ...'

Roy then wondered if it was racist to believe that if there was anything worse than one Irish witness it was three of them!

* * *

A disturbance on the Aylesbury Housing Estate began over a note left affixed to the windscreen of a badly parked car. It read: '*YOU! Through*

75

your careless parking you are blocking our access. Observe the sign under your car, you pratt. NO PARKING!'

On his return, the complainant found the following notice on *his* windscreen: '*YOU! Through your bad language and careless sticking of notes on windscreens, you have left me an open invitation to park here whenever I f.....g WANT!!'*

* * *

PC George Wilkinson had covered the Petticoat Lane market for many years and knew most of the traders well. One Sunday morning there was a disturbance at a fruit stall between a complaining shopper and a buxom stall holder. The main display on the stall was an impressive array of honeydew melons. They were priced cheaply and, at least on first glance, appeared of good quality, although it seemed the shopper did not think so.

As George neared the disputing females, the stall holder thrust out her ample chest and placed her hands defiantly on her hips.

'Georgie, lad,' she exclaimed, obviously delighted to see him. 'You've known me for years, ain't you, son?'

George nodded dutifully.

'Then tell her, will you?' She tilted her head towards the complainant. 'Ain't I known everywhere for having the best quality melons in the market?'

* * *

Sheffield PC listing his actions after being called to a husband-and-wife assault: 'I then took Mrs Blenkinsop into the bathroom where I placed a cold compost on her head.'

* * *

PC George Hogan was called to the suspected death of an elderly lady in Rotherham and broke into the flat by forcing a window. On approaching the bed, he discovered the old girl was simply asleep. He then became undecided as to his next move. If he left via the forced window and the old lady awoke, she would have a shock. On the other hand, if he shook her awake she might well die of fright.

He then found a double-door between the locked street entrance and the flat proper. He stood in the small space and closed the door on himself, knocking his knuckles off in an attempt to wake her.

After ten minutes of slowly weakening knocks, she finally awoke and answered the door, wondering to herself why she had left a policeman in her porch before going to bed.

* * *

I have always been very wary of police first aid. To such an extent that I have often thought it may be better to die with dignity than have some ham-fisted copper bearing down on my pressure-points. It gives me scant satisfaction, though, to say that ex-Sergeant Dan Butson's noble efforts to save life simply bear out my theory.

He had been called with another officer to an old block of flats in Wapping. There, in a top-floor bedroom, a naked middle-aged woman had attempted to gas herself. Such scenes are never pleasant and this one was particularly *un*pleasant. The room was so evil smelling, firstly because of its normal state and secondly because of the uncontrolled body functions of the attempted suicide, that the two policemen decided they could not stay there. Half carrying, half dragging the unconscious female, the pair finally lay her down on the small landing. This being before the 'kiss of life' system of resuscitation, they made the first moves of the Schäfer method. This necessitated firm pressure on the rib-cage. Unfortunately the patient was in such a mess that she slipped clean through their hands and slid down two flights of stairs.

'Well, if she wasn't dead when we started,' commented Dan's colleague, 'she certainly ought to be now.'

But then, to the pair's utter astonishment, a torrent of abuse flooded up from the landing below. The fall had roused her and she was saved!

The only problem was that she was neither happy to be saved nor pleased with the manner in which it was brought about!

* * *

Many police stations keep an index of the tattoos on their villains. Just how comprehensive this is can be gleaned from the arrest of Phillip Wright for assault outside a Chesterfield fish and chip shop. Only minutes before the assault he had dropped his trousers in the shop. He was easily identified by the tattoo on his buttocks.

* * *

PC Dave Springer arrested an Irishman for shoplifting. He had stolen two left shoes of different sizes, one of them with an inbuilt shoe horn. When cautioned, the prisoner replied, 'Well it could have been worse. I might have had a gun.'

* * *

PC Stuart Patt had been part of a cordon at the height of the Tottenham riots. He was shot in the stomach and badly injured. His good friend and best man, Jock Parr, was by his side at the time and also later at the hospital. Stuart's wife was eight and a half months pregnant so Jock also endeavoured to look after her. On the morning after the shooting, Jock had escorted the girl to the hospital and was appalled to see just how ill his friend looked. Pipes, drips and tubes seemed to be everywhere as the victim lay motionless with his eyes closed.

Suddenly there was a flicker of eyelids and Jock saw that his unfortunate friend's gaze seemed to be phrased in a question. Jock bent down over the bed and placed his ear against the panting dry lips. 'Last night,' began the frail voice before trailing off. 'Last night,' it repeated almost as weakly.

'Yes, what is it, Stew? Just take your time, there's a good fellow.'

'Last night ... what time ... was I ... booked off duty?'

'What time?' began Jock in astonishment. 'I'm not sure, but from the time you were shot, I suppose ... half-past eight, wasn't it?'

'Then ...' began the panting policeman as he struggled once more for strength, 'then I'm not on overtime?'

'No, I'm afraid you're not, me old son.'

'Oh shit!' whispered the patient as he slumped back once more into unconsciousness.

* * *

From Ivan St Pierre

An essential accoutrement for all postings to 'Hotel-One' r/t car, at least when Bert Douglas was driving, was a teaspoon (which probably accounts for the force-wide shortage of teaspoons in the canteens of today). No tour of duty would be complete without at least one visit to Tubby Isaacs' Jellied Eel Stall at Aldgate. A carton of eels cost two shillings and sixpence in those days and liberally splashed with spiced vinegar and a lump of ageing bread it made a welcome change from the bangers and mash in the station canteen.

The third member of our car crew was one 'Smudger' Smith, a likeable Devonian with a reputation for exercising his riparian rights whilst on duty. Smudger, with his great knowledge of river life, considered that Tubby was making quite a fortune out of eels. He further offered the opinion that nearby St. Katherine's Dock was full of the things, all alive and eager to be caught.

The next night was Bert's night off. Smudger, determined to create a surprise, arrived with line and bait and promptly requested an early trip to the dock, where he quickly attached a line to a mooring ring. We returned to the scene a few minutes before knocking-off time, where Smudger had pulled from the grimy waters the biggest eel I had ever seen in my life.

My part in this adventure was to deliver the eel to Bert's house on my way home, where he was expected to display his much-boasted culinary art with an old East End recipe. Arriving at the house I received no reply. Not wishing to take the thing home with me – I was, after all, on my way to bed – I began to 'post' it through the letter box. I had about half of it through the slot when the sheer girth of the creature caused it to stick firm. No amount of pushing and pulling would cause it to budge and its slimy coat didn't help. Having little choice, I left the eel half in and half out of the letter box, hoping that the postman would not find it first.

That night, Hotel-One enjoyed fresh local-caught eels for their meal break – and Tubby Isaacs lost seven-and-sixpence in takings.

* * *

Sergeant Joe Smith was attached to West End Central police station and he had a leaning to catch PCs who were absent from their fixed posts, be they security or traffic. One regular offender was a constable of advanced service who, no matter how hard he tried, the strict sergeant could never catch.

One day, whilst the sergeant was making his rounds, he noticed that the fixed point at a particularly busy junction was not covered. 'Got him at last!' Hastening into the nearby section house, he quickly discovered the offending constable supping tea.

'But I'm reporting an accident, Sarge,' protested the old constable in hurt tones.

'Oh, yeah,' reported the disbelieving sergeant. He picked up the accident book and studied the times. Under 'Details of driver' was shown a local telephone number. A little later the sergeant rang the number and was surprised, not to say disappointed, to discover that the PC had been telling the truth concerning the time and place of the accident.

It was at the PC's retirement party a few years later that the truth finally came out.

'Ere, d'you remember when you nearly nailed me down for being off my point, guv?' (The dedicated sergeant was by this time a chief inspector.)

'I do indeed,' muttered the chief inspector. 'And I know to this day you were lying – but everything about that accident book was in order.'

'Not everything, guv,' pointed out the old trooper. 'The signature wasn't, for a start – it wasn't mine! I'd heard you were looking for me, so I bought the "accident" from a young recruit for half-a-quid ... five seconds before you came in the door!'

* * *

The white transit vans that are now so much an integral part of modern-day policing, are known throughout the force as Instant Response Units, or more generally as IRUs. This name was actually the *second* choice, because for the first few weeks of their existence they were officially known as Fast Action Response Transits.

Then someone noticed the abbreviation ...

* * *

The informant on this one, understandably, wishes to remain anonymous.

A rather large constable was on his way back to Kensington police station in the early hours when he found a small, slightly built drunk, flat out in a doorway. Knowing the station van was otherwise engaged, and because of the close proximity of the station, he decided to carry in the prisoner over his shoulder. A few minutes later, he staggered through the back gate and into the charge-room, where he dropped his prisoner into the old wooden armchair. On regaining his breath, he routinely asked, 'Okay, mate, what's your name?'

Mate did not answer – and for the best of reasons.

Mate was dead.

Now, there were two unlucky people there. The corpse and the poor sod who had carried him in. Because now he had to carry him out again. You see if dying in a doorway is unfortunate, dying in a police station is disastrous! Apart from giving the place a bad name, the paperwork is horrendous.

Making sure he was still unobserved, the copper humped the body back over his shoulder and tiptoed out into the street, where he eased it into the deepest doorway he could find.

* * *

Arthur Holmans was posted night-duty area-car in South East London, when around four in the morning, a 'chase' began some few miles away. Now 4am is a very sleepy hour and the chances are that the r/t sets would have been particularly quiet, with few calls being either received or transmitted. The main problem with this boredom is that when a long car chase is on, the bandit vehicle will pick up an additional pursuer for every manor he races through. There is frequently more danger from the following procession of three-litre police cars than ever there is from the bandit himself – as most drivers will testify.

By the time Arthur's car had joined the hunt it was thirteenth in the pecking order and some 25% of the entire Met police's area-cars were following each other at eighty miles per hour down the Old Kent Road. It was soon after this that the bandit car skidded out of control and almost turned over. It was quickly hemmed in by four of the pursuing police vehicles and the lone occupant arrested.

Arthur had left his own car and trotted to the head of the line in case he recognised the driver. He was just in time to see the person being carried struggling and yelling into a police van. Whilst he did not recognise the individual, he certainly recognised the type. The tall, dark, powerfully built young man with an intimidating appearance was very similar to the type Arthur had visualised. Predictable though the prisoner may have been, his threats were proving to be anything but. 'If yer don't let me go,' screamed the hysterical villain, 'I'm goin' ter tell me mum!'

* * *

During the Murdoch-printers' dispute in Wapping in 1986 I had occasion to visit my old police station to see a former colleague. He had returned a few minutes earlier from duty on the printers' picket line.

'What's it like there?' I asked, as a polite conversation opener.

He shrugged. 'Well, they're the best-dressed pickets I've ever seen – all sheepskins, Gucci wellies and brandy fumes.'

* * *

From Alf Henry

The atmosphere within the force becomes particularly relaxed at Christmas. Essential tasks are of course carried out, together with routine matters such as the feeding of prisoners etc. But in the main, no one seeks to carve himself out a career at that time of the year. It was with this knowledge that I began my first Christmas night-duty some thirty years ago. All the sergeants had wangled the evening off and my friend Sid had been promoted to the temporary rank of acting-sergeant. Now there was no point in having your friend as sergeant unless he posted you to the beat nearest your home. It was therefore no surprise to be given 'twelve beat'. After all, I lived in the centre of it.

'I'll tell you what I'll do,' he said. 'I've got to fill in the duty-state, so I'll borrow a bike and join you at your place a bit later on, okay?' It was okay with me. Twelve beat was about forty minutes' walk away, so if he borrowed a bicycle we should both arrive around the same time.

Around about a quarter to eleven, we arrived at my front door in time to join a few friends and relatives in a yuletide drink. The company was convivial and almost before we realised, it was one o'clock.

'Hey, come on!' I said urgently. 'Look at the clock! I know it's Christmas but we must go back to the nick sometime.'

A few minutes later we had said our good-nights and had set off once more for the station. I was to take the most direct route and Sid, because of the bicycle, was taking a longer and more devious route. The only thing that bothered me was that of the group of people we had just left only Sid had been drinking Scotch – and there was only half a bottle left! Still, he appeared to be fine: his speech was certainly clear, he was quite coherent and gave little or no indication that he had been drinking.

I arrived back at the station a little before 2am and fully expected to see the bike propped up in the yard. It was not there; neither was Sid. When he still hadn't arrived by three o'clock I began to worry. I was just thinking of organising a search-party when he turned up – bruised, torn and battered, with the twisted remains of the bicycle slung over his shoulder. In spite of his appearance, he still seemed coherent. Well, if it wasn't caused by the drink how *was* it caused? Was it a hit-and-run? Had he stumbled across a robbery? Just what had happened? I asked.

'Well,' he muttered, appearing reluctant to even give a reason. 'I was riding down Doddington Grove, which as you know is the widest street on the manor – yes?'

I nodded.

'Well, I was riding down Doddington Grove –'

'You've just said that.'

'Well, I was riding down Doddington Grove and I thought ...' His voice drifted away to a whisper. 'I wonder how far I can ride this bike with my eyes shut.'

* * *

PCs Les Davenport and Steve Burgess attended a crime inquiry to deal with a criminal damage to a front door. Whilst at the premises, they saw what appeared to be a pocket calculator attached to the inside of the door. After rashly asking the occupier to explain its use, they spent the next fifteen minutes listening to him explain that it was the most advanced audible alarm in existence.

'For twenty-eight quid,' the man claimed, 'it was an absolute bargain!' He said he had had a previous alarm of the same make but it had proved to be faulty. This one, though, was the real business. He was so pleased and proud of the thing that he offered a demonstration. Leaving the two constables inside, he stepped outside the premises and closed the door. No sooner did he touch the door than the alarm screamed into life. This carried on for three or four minutes, during which time Les and Steve felt they were going mad. The occupier, who then returned to the premises, spent the next few minutes frantically trying to stop it. He claimed the actual alarm was fine – it was the door that was faulty.

He tapped out the secret code but the alarm, if anything, increased in volume. He thumped the thing frantically, again without improvement. Swearing profusely, he ripped it from the wall, leaving the wires and components still stuck to the door. Still it wailed.

Now desperate, the occupier rushed into the bathroom and plunged the thing into a wash-basin of water. The alarm gave one last wail before dying under a deluge of bubbles. Turning to the two constables, he sobbed, 'My wife will kill me for this!'

Leaving the wires hanging, the alarm bubbling and the occupier in tears, Les and Steve tiptoed quietly out.

* * *

Most cops-and-robbers films finish with an inevitable car chase and a dramatic last scene shoot-out before the villain is finally apprehended. PC Dave Biss's arrest of a felon also incorporated a late-stage car chase but the dramatic use of guns was avoided. Dave's system was much more effective – although as potentially dangerous.

The bandit had raced his car into a cul-de-sac. Although he could no longer escape with the vehicle, he could still make it on foot – there was an alley leading from the end of the cul-de-sac into a nearby housing estate. Even though his pursuer was fairly close, he now had an excellent chance to make his escape. Dave realised this only too well and knew if he was to have any chance of arresting the man then he would need to display some very smart footwork – not Dave's strongest point.

The chase had been fairly even so far; the bandit's car was a rather clapped-out but still quite lively Ford, whilst the pursuing police car was just a small general-purpose runaround that had suffered too many drivers. As the quarry skidded to a halt in the middle of the road, the driver was away and out of the car almost before the wheels had ceased turning. If Dave was to have any chance at all then he needed to be just as speedy. He certainly had the door open quick enough and, as he knocked the automatic lever into neutral, he bounded quickly from his seat. Unfortunately our hero did not bound very far. About thirty-six inches to be precise.

Throughout the chase, Dave's personal radio had lain on the front passenger seat and he had professionally swept it up in one smooth movement as he leaped from the car. Well actually he wasn't all *that* professional because the strap of the radio had become looped around the gear lever. This sudden action promptly pulled the lever back into 'drive'. Being an automatic car with engine still running, that is exactly what happened – it *drove*. Straight into a builder's skip laden with rubble.

The instant yell of agony emitted by the policeman had little to do with any injury he may have, or was about to sustain. But it had everything to do with the visions of long weeks of report writing in which he attempted to explain how a driverless police car collided with a stationary builder's skip in a cul-de-sac during a chase in which the prisoner escaped on foot.

It was at this last despairing stage that the fates changed to the side of the good guy. If Charlie 'Hot-rod' Kirton, who was a fairly successful car thief, had a weakness at all, it was his almost insatiable curiosity. The scream, combined with the crash, proved all too much for his rubber-necked qualities. Even though sprinting flat out, he just couldn't resist a quick glance back at the pandemonium he had caused. I think Charlie actually thought that the lamp-post had deliberately stepped out in front of him. Whatever the reason, the pair of them collided with a sickening thud that laid him out for some five minutes.

The effect of poor Charlie's misfortune on David was remarkable. He was instantly much cheerier. It is truly amazing just how much of an accident can be squared up when the villain is nicked.

* * *

During the reconstruction of central Croydon a great many buildings were either demolished, altered or extended. In almost every street there was at least one construction site.

At the junction of Wellesley Road and North Street, for example, there must have been a building of some considerable stature, because after the demolition men had moved on, all that remained was a solitary reminder of the junction's former glory. It was a great white stone angel with a large pair of stone wings. The face was kindly yet firm and it stared protectively away into the middle distance.

The Croydon night-duty were sad to see the statue relegated to such a menial fate. One boring Monday it was decided to elect it as the new patron saint for bus travellers. A few industrious coppers soon deposited it at the head of the nearby bus queue where, in the midst of an extremely busy shopping area, it was to remain, until appearing on the front page of a newspaper several days later.

Coming as it had, mysteriously in the night, London Transport had taken no chances, doubtless figuring they needed all the help they could get.

* * *

It is strange how some things upset certain people yet others are unmoved by them. Take market stalls, for instance. A fairly innocuous commodity, but a certain sergeant at Croydon would work himself up to a high degree of indignation every time the traders in the street market left their stalls out overnight. Now, strictly speaking, they should not have done this, and it was certainly in breach of the bye-laws, but it saved them time in the mornings and there were other things for the police to concern themselves about. (Stone angels for example!!) Unfortunately, whenever this particular sergeant was on night-duty he would insist that the PCs fetch the stalls into the station where, next morning, the traders would pay to have them restored.

Now pushing stalls around in the early hours was not amongst the favourite tasks of the constables. It was therefore suggested to the sergeant that perhaps the police van, under the careful control of Charlie Northeast, could attend and, bearing in mind the streets were deserted, tow them all to the station in one trip. Whilst the sergeant was not too keen on the idea, he reluctantly agreed.

'Well, all right,' he said grudgingly. 'But for Gawd's sake, take it easy, Charlie, I don't want any Brand's Hatch approaches to the bends.'

'Don't you worry, Sarge,' Charlie assured him. 'I'll creep along so slow you won't notice I'm moving.'

So the van attended and with a few yards of rope and a chorus of 'Wagons ... row-hole!' six stalls trundled slowly along the High Street.

Now it is at this stage that my informants become devious. The questions seem to be: (1) Did the rope break? (2) Was the rope cut? Or (3) Was it simply not tied correctly? Whatever the reason, the last stall slipped its moorings and gathered momentum down the hill, finally coming to rest in the plate-glass window of a shoe-shop. The owner of the store was not amused. The stall holder was not amused. The sergeant was sick and the constables bewildered (well *most* of them were).

But as Charlie rightly said, 'Every cloud has a silver lining,' and strange to relate, the stalls were never fetched into the station again.

* * *

Arthur Dawes, a retired PC from South London, wrote about a Wimbledon tennis tournament that he covered during his time in the force. He had watched with interest as a party of Chelsea pensioners, resplendent in their scarlet tunics, had gathered together for some obviously intended function.

Standing alongside Arthur, and watching with even greater interest, was an Australian tourist.

'The corks weren't actually swinging from his hat,' said Arthur, 'but everything else about him was straight out of a lager commercial. Anyway, he stared open mouthed at the old fellows for some seconds, then, shaking his head in wonderment, he turned to me and said, "Jesus, Officer, but that's a bloody old band!"'

* * *

From the Warren *magazine*

Mr John Thoroughgood had his car stolen. It was subsequently found and taken into the yard at a South London police station.

Mr Thoroughgood was informed of his good fortune and the following evening he arrived with his friend, Reuben O'Driscoll, who waited in his car outside the station. When Mr Thoroughgood went to start his car he discovered the petrol tank was empty. He then went out to his friend Reuben and asked him to pop along to a nearby garage to purchase a gallon. At the garage, following Reuben's request for a gallon of three star, the attendant pointed out that it would be of great help if Reuben had something to put it in. After a quick rummage around, Reuben came up with the only thing in his car that could remotely carry petrol: a wellington boot. This was reluctantly topped up by a more than apprehensive attendant.

Meanwhile, back at the police station, PC Fred Carstairs drove a panda car into the yard and left it in a parking bay at an angle. About the same time Inspector Mark Levenson was driving to the station to report for duty.

With his wellington boot full of petrol, Reuben left the garage and returned to his friend by driving into the back yard of the station, neatly ignoring the 'Authorised Police Vehicles Only' sign at the entrance. On his arrival in the yard, he was surprised not to find his friend John. In order to save time, Reuben rather considerately decided to pour the petrol in for him.

It was at that moment that Mr John Thoroughgood returned to the yard and wondered just why his friend Reuben should be putting petrol in a police car. Too late he screamed a warning.

At that moment Inspector Levenson drove into the yard and was confronted by an Englishman shouting at an Irishman who was pouring petrol into a police car, using a wellington boot. This so distracted him (a Scot) that he drove straight into the panda car that PC Carstairs had left so badly parked.

Of course the resulting report of this accident caused the most predictable of circulars to be urgently teleprinted to all stations: 'The practice of allowing persons to carry quantities of petrol in wellington boots whilst on police premises must cease forthwith.'

* * *

From Bruce Baker
One day, whilst I was on duty outside Buckingham Palace, an obvious nutter approached my colleague and me, stating he had an appointment to see Princess Anne. He was asked to produce his authorisation but of course could not. He then asked where he could obtain such authorisation and, to get rid of him, we told him, 'From the officer on duty in Trafalgar Square.' (There were always three on duty at all times in those days.) We assured him that they would give him all the necessary documents with no problems at all. He wandered off quite happily, and we thought smugly that we had seen the last of him.

Imagine our dismay when, some time later, he returned flourishing a slip of official police memo paper, bearing the words:

> *To you at the Palace from us at the Square:*
> *Please admit the bearer to Buckingham Palace*
> *for an audience with the Princess Anne.*

* * *

From Reg Taylor

In the early hours of a summer morning, I was driving Zulu 3, which was the Croydon area-car, together with Lofty Bullock, my r/t operator, and Don Lees, my plain-clothes observer. We heard a call go to neighbouring Zulu 4 concerning a disturbance in a petrol station. Apparently a slightly inebriated West Indian had insisted on serenading the pump attendant with his guitar. Having no musical ear, the pump attendant had, after three-quarters of an hour of unrelenting calypsos, understandably set his dog on the serenader. The singer had sustained a slight tear to his trousers and an even slighter graze to his left testicle. Neither appeared to be very serious and after a brief discussion he was pointed down the road and sent on his melodic away.

It was half an hour before the singer decided that his injury merited a little more police attention than had so far been shown. By this time he had crossed the border line of the manor. It was therefore our car that received the emergency call from the roadside telephone box. 'See informant re assault,' was the brief message from the radio room at Scotland Yard.

Perhaps it was because the effects of the drink had worn off, but the former cheery troubadour had now changed into a rather belligerent complainant. 'I've been castrated by a wild animal, that's what I've been, and I want to see a doctor!' was his opening demand.

'Well, let's have a look first,' I said.

'No! I want a doctor. It's my right and I'm not going anywhere until I get one.'

At this time Don Lees, who so far that night had been anything *but* observing, was slumped asleep on the back seat of the police car. However, Lofty Bullock was quick to realise that the cause of Don's exhaustion (he had played cricket all day instead of sleeping) could also be our salvation. Coming as he had straight from the match, the team's cricket gear was now in the boot of the area-car, together with the umpire's white coat.

'Oi! Wake up!' hissed Lofty into the slumbering observer's ear.

'Wassamarrer, wassamarrer?'

'You're now a doctor, that's wassamarrer. Get the umpire's coat on and examine that black bloke's knackers.'

Now any constable who is in the habit of sleeping in the back of an area-car must, of necessity, expect to wake instantly into a variety of changing and even dramatic circumstances. But to be ordered to don an umpire's white coat and scrutinise the scrotum of an angry black stranger was unusual, even by night-duty police car standards.

'But –'

'Don't argue, just *do* it!'

'But what exactly do I *do*?'

'Just lift them up and tell him they're okay. That's all he needs – reassurance. *You'd* need reassurance if a bloody great Alsatian had grabbed your bollocks!' he added sympathetically.

It was just as well that it was still dark because the general condition of the umpire's coat left a great deal to be desired. However, the idea seemed to work and within a minute or so, the complainant was sitting sideways in the driver's seat with his legs outside the car and his trousers around his ankles. Don meanwhile was gingerly lifting the patient's genitals with a blue biro pen. I was watching the examination with only mild interest when the first filtering notes of an undecipherable tune began. Lofty had apparently always nursed a desire to play the guitar. He was now perched happily on the wing of the car trying to pick out scales.

It was, I suppose, predictable that Zulu 4 would choose that precise moment to see if we needed a hand with our 'assault'.

As the driver of Zulu 4 said later, 'When you go to an emergency call at half past three in the morning, you don't really expect to see one uniformed copper sitting on the bonnet of a police car strumming a guitar and another examining the testicles of a complainant. Particularly one that you've recently classified as having "No need for police action".'

* * *

From ex-PC George Hinkling

During the late 1950s we had a highly respected but extremely strict superintendent, aptly named Bert Standfast, in charge of our station. Although well liked, Bert was a great disciplinarian and almost paranoiac about his men drinking on duty.

One Saturday morning, a new shoe-shop opened in the High Street and the proprietor had arranged a 'celebrity opening'. The lady who was to perform this task was a stunning statuesque blonde who was at the time performingly weekly in a top-rated TV series called 'The Army Game'. Crowds began to assemble outside the shop long before the lady was due to arrive. Myself and fellow constable Ian Hanson were therefore sent along to the premises to generally keep order and the footway clear. This was not too arduous a task as everybody was extremely good natured. Excellent business was done by Abe Fertleman the proprietor, and once matters had quietened he invited Ian and myself, together with the luscious starlet, into his back room for a 'wee one'.

Now I am not over tall, barely five feet nine and a half, but Ian was at least an inch or so less and his barrel-like build caused him to appear even shorter. Whether it was the attraction of opposites I really can't say, but he became instantly smitten by the tall blonde. She appeared a friendly enough girl and after the four of us had made a considerable hole in a bottle of Scotch, Ian's normal shy reticence gave way to a more cheery, expansive demeanour than I ever knew he possessed.

'How about a couple of snaps – for the family album, y'know?' asked Abe, holding up his camera.

'O'course, why not?' we enthused as we beamed our alcoholic smiles into the lens.

It was the following week that I next patrolled that part of the manor. My mind was in neutral as I strolled along at the regulation three miles an hour.

'It's 'im! It's 'im! I told yer!' exclaimed an elderly passing shopper to her companion. I looked around with mild interest to see just who 'im might be but I appeared the only male for some distance. The matter had almost slipped from my mind when another pair of shoppers stared at me then nudged each other knowingly. By this time I had almost reached the shoe-shop and I thought that if Abe was anywhere to be seen I would wave an acknowledgement. His shop window seemed particularly popular that morning, with several people staring first into the glass, then after a quick side glance at me straight back into the window again.

'Smashin' picture of you, mate,' said a tired old blonde with two shopping bags, nodding towards the display of high heels and slingbacks.

'Eh? Where?'

She put down one bag and pointed. Following the direction of her finger I closed my eyes in horror. There in the centre of the show display was an enlarged black-and-white picture measuring some twenty-four inches square. It was illuminated by a powerful spotlight set high above the corner of the window. The picture was a crystal-clear reproduction of two short, bleary-eyed, helmetless coppers on either side of a towering blonde. One of the constables (me) was raising his glass in salute to the camera and the other had his arms locked around the waist of the busty young miss, with his forehead covered in lipstick and an adoring soppy smile on his face. A police helmet was perched saucily on the back of the blonde's head.

'Great picture, George, ennit?' called the nasal voice of Abe Fertleman. 'Your mate seems to be doin' all right,' he added with a knowing wink.

'Great pic— ! What the bloody hell are you trying to do, Abe? Get us the sack? Get it out, for God's sake!'

Abe was not at all happy about losing his sales promotion and reluctantly agreed to do so only after I bought the picture from him for the fiver that he claimed it cost. As five pounds consisted of two-thirds of my week's wages, I considered the three pounds ten shillings I claimed from Ian was by no means exorbitant.

The picture, meanwhile, some thirty years later, still lies at the bottom of my wardrobe. On the rare occasions I get it out, I feel that old Bert Standfast gives another involuntary jerk in his grave.

* * *

PC Reg Taylor had what he at least considered an undeserved reputation for trouble. Whether it was sheer bad luck or just pure cussedness no one could say for sure, but it was an undeniable fact that whenever he was involved in an incident, then someone, either police or prisoner, would wind up thumped.

Sergeant Bill Johnson had made it quite clear that he considered it was now high time for Reg to mend his ways. 'Let's see if we can go a whole week without some poor sod collecting a fat lip, shall we, Taylor? If not, there had better be a bloody good reason for it,' he threatened darkly.

The above conversation had taken place at 3pm on a Monday at the start of a week's late-turn duty. Six hours later the charge-room door burst open and Reg was to be seen leading in a struggling prisoner with a bloodied nose that now covered half of his face. The old sergeant could restrain himself no longer. 'What the bleedin' hell did I tell you, Taylor? You've gone too far this time. I warned you only this afternoon and here you are already at it again! You had better just have one hell of a good story, that's all I can say.'

'Sarge,' sighed Reg sadly, 'I know you ain't going to believe it but it honestly wasn't my fault and I didn't do it.'

'Who did this to you, mate?' the sergeant asked the now slumped prisoner. The prisoner turned his head towards Reg. 'He did,' he announced wearily.

'Ah ha! So it *wasn't* you, eh, Taylor?'

'Nah, Sarge,' said the prisoner. 'It wasn't 'im. It was '*im*.' He pointed just beyond the protesting constable to where a newcomer had just entered the room – a frail, bespectacled elderly newcomer, with a vicar's collar and an arm that was swathed in a bloodstained plaster-of-paris.

It subsequently transpired that the local church were running a fundraising week and a few members of the parish were assisting on various stalls and at the refreshment bar. The prisoner, an eighteen-year-old tattooed skinhead, had been one of a gang of six who had done their best to ruin the whole thing. He had overturned a couple of stalls and managed to give a middle-aged lady assistant a swift kicking before running out into the mid-November evening.

The vicar, who had sustained a broken arm some weeks before, was furious and had chased the raiders into the street, where he soon lost them. On the arrival of the police, Reg offered the vicar a seat in the rear of the car whilst a search was carried out. The gang were soon spotted but once more made their escape, with the exception of the one who had kicked the lady helper. He was arrested and placed in the rear of the area-car, with Reg positioned between him and the vicar.

En route to the station, the vicar tried to remonstrate with the lad but was soon told to 'Shut your face, you old pratt!' It was all too much for the reverend gentleman. Instinctively and like lightning he swung a thin but well-plastered arm three times across the front of his police minder and smack into the face of his tormentor. The predictable squeals from the skinhead were only matched by the instant remorse of the vicar. He appeared dumbfounded by his own aggression. If the mortification of the man of God cut little ice with the spotty youth, it cut even less with the older constable. After all, who would now believe that the exploded nose was caused not by the pugnacious copper but by a frail, elderly, one-armed vicar?

Well, not Sergeant Johnson, for one.

Traffic Patrol

The removal squad were clearing a street of offending vehicles that were parked on double-yellow lines. Eventually they reached a rusty clapped-out old Daf. Unbeknown to the officer removing the car, the Daf is one of the few automatic vehicles that will actually start 'in gear'. After a quick jiggle with his master keys, the ignition leaped into life. Unfortunately the ignition was not the only thing that leaped – the car did, too. Straight into the rear of a brand new Mercedes, causing £6,000 worth of damage.

Suddenly a window cleaner appeared out of nowhere and pointed furiously at the Daf. 'My guv'nor's going to have the right hump with you!' he exclaimed. 'He's just paid forty quid for that.'

* * *

A heavily laden open-back lorry was removed from a West London clearway and throughout the journey to the pound the removal officer was aware of a persistent knocking. As he finally drove into the gates, an upside-down face appeared at the top of his windscreen. It was the lorry-driver who had been on the load adjusting his ropes.

* * *

A middle-aged lady went to the car-pound at Hyde Park to reclaim her vehicle. The pound is located beneath the park and the unfortunate woman was claustrophobic. Within a few minutes the confined space caused her to become totally hysterical and an ambulance was sent for.

A young PC at the pound, having recently passed his first aid exam, finally managed to calm the lady and the ambulance was sent away. Suitably soothed, she was given a cup of tea and directed to the claimants' counter. Her new-found composure instantly vanished when she discovered how much it was going to cost her. She was promptly hysterical again and the same ambulance returned.

* * *

The first time the removal officer knew there was a baby in the back of the estate car that he had just driven to the pound, was when a call came out – 'to a kidnapping!'

* * *

From Colin Hobday
The old traffpol had a young recruit posted to the car for a few days in order for him to gain experience. They stopped a real heap of a car in the shape of an old Ford Cortina. The car had seemed to knock and wobble over every yard it travelled.

The eager young man was out of the police car and under the engine of the Ford almost before the wheels had ceased moving. After a few minutes he emerged triumphantly and claimed he had found the cause of the noise. What he had failed to find, however, was the cracked feed pipe that had seeped engine oil over the front of his tunic. The old traffpol pointed at the tunic and said jokingly to the rather large lady driver, 'Under the terms of the Act, you're obliged to wash that lot.'

The lady studied the young man for a second, then, shrugging her powerful shoulders, said, 'Okay, but how do I get him in my machine?'

* * *

From Graham Batho
The young traffic policeman was riding north in Park Lane on a hot

summer's morning when he spied a young lady in hotpants beside a Mini that had obviously broken down. This is a situation that most traffpols dream about. It's like rescuing the damsel from the dragon. Doing a swift U-turn he pulled up smoothly alongside the harassed maiden and offered to find the fault. After the briefest of examinations, he easily found the cause of her trouble. 'You've got a flat battery,' he announced. 'Oh really,' she replied with some interest. 'What shape should it be?'

* * *

Three young traffpol motorcyclists were assigned to escort an unusually large load. This consisted of a large pull-and-push low loader with a super-duper multi-million-pound yacht for delivery to the East India Docks. The yacht was built into a large cradle, resulting in the deck and cabin being well over the height of a London transport double-decker bus. The route was carefully chosen to avoid bridges and other low projections. On arriving at the dock, the load had to travel down a narrow road with tall blocks of flats on either side. This road was only wide enough for one vehicle to move at a time and the load came to a standstill while the dock gates were unlocked. The occupants of the third- and fourth-floor flats could, had they been so inclined, have stepped straight out onto the deck of the yacht.

Due to the noise and excitement, a lady occupant of one of the ground-floor flats in this otherwise quiet and peaceful cul-de-sac of the East End, came to the door in curlers, slippers and dressing-gown.

Young traffpol motorcyclist, never one to miss such an opportunity, turns to the lady and enquires, 'D'you order a boat from Janet Frazer?'

'No I f...ing didn't!' says she, as she turns on her heels and slams the door.

* * *

The traffic patrol removed a caravanette that had been causing obstruction in a quiet side road in the West End. About halfway to the car pound, the removal officer was compelled to stop at the traffic lights. A young man and lady, in various stages of undress, then emerged from the darkness at the rear of the van and enquired if the ride would take long.

* * *

From Clearway *Traffic Patrol Magazine*
Two very experienced traffic patrol officers (who certainly should have known better!) found themselves on the opposite side of the river Thames to their garage and with a falling fuel gauge. With crossed fingers they chanced the Blackwall tunnel and halfway through they received their just deserts when the Landrover spluttered to a standstill. Realising they would be ribbed unmercifully, to say nothing about committing an offence under the by-laws, they decided to look for a suitable samaritan to tow them out of the tunnel.

Almost the first vehicle they saw looked very suspicious indeed. In fact it wasn't just suspicious – it was stolen! Arresting the occupants, they then harnessed the stolen vehicle to the fuelless Landrover and towed it to the nearest police station. There the villains were charged – and a discreet gallon of petrol purchased.

Phew!

* * *

A dramatic request was received in the traffic garage for some emergency lighting and half a dozen shovels. This equipment was to be conveyed post-haste to an East London riverbank where a witness had just seen three men fill in a grave.

A quick inspection of the location confirmed very recent digging and new-laid turves. The eager team of best-suited detectives were then handed the shovels and went to work with zeal.

An hour or so later, at the bottom of the six-feet grave, they found the very same gas main that the three 'suspects' had just repaired.

* * *

For the Metropolitan Police Traffic Patrol, it really had been 'one of those mornings'. Everything that could go wrong with London's traffic had *gone* wrong – and with a vengeance. Wheels had come off, traffic lights had failed, water mains had burst and lorry loads slipped. In addition to all this the computer was 'down' and some cretin had just given the commander apoplexy by playing a bugle over the force radio. It was also raining.

It was against this background that the new traffpol officer found himself on a solo motorcycle in the middle of Hyde Park Corner doing his best to assist the thousands of crawling motorists. Sod's Law once more played its hand and there, right in the worst possible place, a young lady's car broke down. The officer, true to his calling, remained calm and rendered such assistance as was required to get the car moving again.

As soon as this was accomplished, another vehicle broke down, almost in the same spot. Still undaunted, the officer sighed and walked the few yards to assist the second driver. As he reached this second unfortunate, he suddenly realised that his crash-helmet was on the back seat of the first car. There, at nine in the morning, at Hyde Park Corner and improperly dressed, he turned to catch the young lady before she drove away.

Too late! Still, the sweet young thing did acknowledge his wave before she roared happily off in one of the few moving lanes of the morning. This did present a problem. As we know, the officer had no helmet, but in addition, he was now stuck with a solo motorcycle that he could no longer ride because he had no helmet!

Well, there was nothing to be gained by self-pity, so he turned his attention to the second car. After a few minutes our wizard managed his second noble deed of the morning, as that car too burst into life. Not only that, but at the same moment he heard on his radio that the young lady driver had just deposited his crash-helmet at Bow Street!

Now almost out of the wood, our hero mounted his machine and went to put on his gauntlets ... His gauntlets? Oh yes, his gauntlets. Well, you see they were in the back of the second vehicle – and have not been seen since.

* * *

'But officer,' panted the eye-fluttering young thing in her open-top MG sports. 'I thought you *never* reported the pretty ones.'

'You are *so* right, madam! ... You are not obliged to say anything ...'

* * *

The following dialogue recently took place over traffic patrol's r/t wavelength. ('Oscar' being the traffic control's r/t call sign.)

Quebec-17: 'Oscar, for your information, a mist or fog has descended on the Greenford flyover.'

Oscar: 'Very well, Quebec-17. What is the total visibility?'

Q17: 'It's down to a hundred yards.'

Oscar: 'And the tailback?'

Q17: 'Well it's at least a hundred yards.'

* * *

From Colin Hobday

A traffpol motorcyclist sat dozily on his machine whilst waiting for the traffic lights to change. As the amber lit up, he prepared for the 'off'. Suddenly his attention was drawn to the side road where a fast-moving van was obviously going to chance a 'late red'. The van-driver then seemed to see the policeman about the same time.

Considering just how late he had left it, he made a rather brave attempt to brake. Sadly it didn't work. The van came to a stop three-quarters across the junction in a tyre-burning, smoke-filled halt that coincided with a resounding clatter of glass.

'What've you got in the back, mate?' asked the policeman curiously.

'Dresden china, Dartington glass – and my resignation, no doubt,' said the unfortunate driver.

* * *

One dark Friday evening, traffic was heavily congested in Regent Street with late-night shoppers thronging pavements and crossing places. Outside Hamleys a large French motor-coach seemed to have been abandoned and traffic was slowly grinding to a halt.

Now large foreign motor-coaches are not the simplest of things in the world to operate. First of all they have scores of controls and, secondly, few of them are labelled in English. It was therefore with some trepidation and no little courage that the two officers from traffic patrol decided it had to be moved. They approached the driver's door with jigglers and window spanners poised.

Already there was the feel of challenge in the air. A crowd was assembling steadily in the obvious expectation of a drama – they were not to be disappointed.

The first officer began to work on the lock with such vigour and enthusiasm that when it burst open it did so to loud applause. This applause caused the crowd to grow faster as scores gathered round for an even better view. Once inside, our heroes clambered into the driver's seat and attacked the ignition lock. Would the ignition prove a bigger challenge than the door? No! this too yielded to our experts, as the dashboard lit up into a display of flashing and different coloured lights. Soon every interior light came on as laughter and yet more applause came from the assembled throng. For the two heroes, though, there still remained the most difficult obstacle of all: the ignition sequence. Like two musicians on an electric keyboard, their fingers were a blur as they pushed, pulled and switched every control in sight. The coach in its turn responded magnificently. Doors opened and closed, with rushes of compressed air, seats reclined, pre-recorded tour information blared out, music played and the air-conditioning motor whined. Everything seemed to work except that little spark that would galvanise the huge engine into life. Well, actually there was one other control that they had first of all missed. But then they found it! Could it be the the one they so keenly sought?

Suddenly panic gripped the uninvited audience. Women screamed, children cried and grown men beat a hasty retreat. Looking down from their lofty position, the two traffpols saw people clutching their handkerchiefs to their faces and throwing off their contaminated clothing. Yes, that's right! Our two lads had just discharged fifty gallons of air-assisted chemical toilet contents across their previously admiring fans! In the resulting chaos there was nothing left to do but melt sadly away into the night.

*　*　*

From Colin Hobday

Slight bumper-to-bumper accidents are not required to be reported to police and in fact are not welcomed. Personal injury accidents, however, must be reported. It was therefore with some surprise that the crew of Oscar Golf One-five received a call to a personal injury accident in which one car was completely unscathed, the other had a scratch on the bumper that could be removed with a rag – yet blood absolutely *covered* the front two seats of the car.

The source of the blood was only too obvious. The second driver's nose was split from top to bottom.

'How on earth did this happen, mate?' asked the bemused traffic patrol.

'Well,' said the driver tearfully. 'I was creeping along in slow-moving traffic when the car in front stopped suddenly and we just nudged bumpers.'

'So?'

'Well ... you see, I was picking me nose at the time ...'

*　*　*

From Colin Hobday

A certain young traffpol, a frail pale youth, barely out of his teens, was posted night-duty communications officer. Now, busy though traffic patrol may be during the day, the communications officer had little to do after midnight except answer the telephone. He therefore set a few hours aside to renew the brake system on his car. This is a task that will take some considerable time, especially when attempted alone. Nothing daunted, he secreted the car in the corner of the garage so he could continue the task the following night.

After the third night of arduous toil, the traffpol had finished and, to his credit, the brakes worked perfectly. His hands, however, were as black as Newgate's Knocker and he set forth to clean them with the special gunge that was kept in a basement washroom. The washroom, though small and obscure, was sufficiently close to the telephone for the user to keep in touch. After scrubbing for some fifteen minutes the hands were perfect. However, they must have been a little slippery, for when he went to replace his engagement ring, it slipped down the overflow pipe.

Annoying? Yes, but no real problem to a lad who had just replaced his entire braking system. He therefore duly took off the 'U' bend, hoping the ring would drop out. That certainly sounded quick but, in fact, it took some considerable time because of the years of paint applications that had seized it solid. Peering up the hole that reeked of generations of nasties, he was horrified to see that his ring was stuck up inside the pipe, with a gap of only three-quarters of an inch between the overflow pipe and the plughole. He could not reach the ring by putting his finger down the overflow pipe but he thought he might just reach it from beneath and thereby push it back up with his finger.

He struggled away for some ten minutes before realising that his finger was now well and truly stuck. It wasn't only stuck but painfully swollen as well. Sitting on the wet floor, he pulled harder and harder but the only result was a fatter and more painful finger. He poured soapy water down the sink but all that did was to raise the water level around his already soggy private parts. He thought of screaming for the sergeant but he decided he couldn't face the humiliation. He even thought of smashing the sink from around his finger. Gritting his teeth and closing his eyes, he gave one last gigantic pull. All that happened was that his finger bled. At this final injury he decided to face the ridicule. He took a deep breath for the scream of all screams – and his finger slipped out, easily and unannounced. Much relieved, he administered first aid by binding the flaking flesh, and as he did so his eyes alighted upon a wire coathanger dangling from a nearby coathook.

This was no *ordinary* wire coathanger, oh dear me no. This was a wire coathanger that seemed to have been placed upon the earth for the sole function of fishing little engagement rings out of sink-holes.

107

Just a gentle poke and within a second it was out; simple.

Returning to the office some two agonising hours after he had left it, he hadn't even been missed.

* * *

In the early hours of one late-spring morning, Kevin Bowsher and his partner, also named Kevin, were on patrol in the district accident car. This is a vehicle specially equipped to deal with serious accidents and suchlike. At exactly 3.05am they arrested a man for drunken driving and took him to Bow Road police station. On their arrival, they were asked to leave the prisoner in the charge-room and go at once to a fatal accident in which a man had been killed.

The accident had taken place close to the location of their drunk-driving arrest. The accident was timed by the ambulance crew as exactly 3.05 am and the victim's name was Death – *Kevin* Death!

'We drove very, very carefully for the rest of that night, I can tell you!' said Kevin unnecessarily.

* * *

Like everything else in recent years, the Metropolitan Police Traffic Patrol has experienced its fair share of cutbacks. Each district garage therefore was required to return part of its stock of motorcycles. Amongst this surplus was an extremely smart BMW.

Having cast covetous eyes over the machine, the garage inspector, a man of considerable knowledge, enquired of a passing constable as to its exact ownership.

'I'm afraid I don't know, sir,' apologised the young man. 'But a bike like that must be well spoken for.'

Undaunted the inspector scoured the machine for some clue as to its current allegiance. 'Here it is,' he said apprehensively as he pointed to a pair of small stickers. He squinted for a moment as he read the tiny print. 'Blast! It's still allocated.' Bending closer he announced, 'It's either Foxtrot 30 or Romeo 32.' He thought deeply for a moment before continuing. 'I can't place either of those two units. Who are they?'

'Tyre pressures, sir,' answered the bland-faced constable.

* * *

From Bruce Baker

A rather beautiful Rolls Royce used to park regularly in Hammersmith Broadway with a large Rottweiler dog obsessively guarding the interior. This proved an extremely effective deterrent for the vehicle removal squad, which in turn caused an enormous amount of obstruction to the flow of traffic in that area.

This frustration continued until the day when a PC arrived with a large bar of Ex-Lax chocolate. This was fed to the dog through the partially opened window and the Rolls Royce was never seen there again.

* * *

From Bruce Baker

One day whilst on traffic patrol we stopped the Landrover to assist a disabled driver in his little blue Invacar. The thing was beyond our repair, so we gave the old boy a lift home. We then returned to the vehicle to tow it to his house, where a mechanic was due to repair it.

As we were hitching it up, I noticed a lady standing in a doorway staring at us. Curiosity, or more like anger, overcame her because she suddenly stormed across the road and demanded to know what we were doing. Then without pausing for breath, or waiting for a reply, she began to harangue us for, as she put it, being heartless and cruel by removing a poor disabled person's car.

She carried on in this vein for some time and finished by saying she was going to telephone the station to complain.

We both stood with blank faces during this tirade and it gave me the most exquisite pleasure to finally explain our actions. Her face was a picture. Needless to say she didn't apologise.

* * *

Traffic motorcyclist Michael Girdlestone was patrolling in the Enfield area one morning when he noticed a man driving a rather luxurious limousine in a line of slow-moving traffic. His attention was understandably drawn because the fellow was eating a slice of toast which he had just taken from a plate that was perched precariously on the dashboard.

The driver was full of apologies and explained that he was very late for a vital business appointment and could, *if there were no more delays*, just make it.

'Have you come far, sir?' asked Mike.

'About twelve miles,' answered the man.

'And do you have far to go?'

'About another six.'

'I see,' murmured Michael thoughtfully. 'There is just one more thing, though, sir.'

'And that is?' responded the man irritably, with an anxious glance at his watch.

'*Why* are you wearing fluffy carpet slippers?'

The tycoon glanced rapidly down at his feet and closed his eyes in disbelief. 'Oh shit.'

* * *

From Mr N.J. Lee

The traffic patrol motorcyclist took up his position outside the great exhibition hall during the Festival of Britain on the South Bank in 1951. His duties were concerned with traffic, both wheeled and pedestrian, in the vicinity of the two main entrances.

It was about midday when he first saw a middle-aged man weaving towards one of these entrances. He was unable to take two steps in a straight line and was muttering weird and strange sounds, more painful than melodious, and occasionally colliding with passers-by. Finally reaching the main entrance, he did a bit of a war dance and promptly flopped on his backside on the pavement. There he sat just swaying around and at one point lay full-length on the pavement. The PC finally decided it was time he did something and radioed for the police van. In the meantime he thought he would keep a low profile by leaving the man where he sat.

As the minutes passed, a taxi pulled in to the kerb right alongside the drunk. A young woman stepped out of the cab and actually had to step over his legs in order to pay the driver. While this was taking place, the drunk crawled on his hands and knees into the back of the cab and, before the cop could dismount from his motorcycle, the driver slammed the passenger door and drove off.

'Okay,' said the van driver irritably. 'I ain't got all day. Where's the drunk?'

'Well ... I don't quite know how to tell you this,' said the traffic cop thoughtfully. 'But he's escaped in a taxi.'

'He's what?'

'Yeah, I know what you're thinking but if you imagine how that cabbie's going to feel when he finds out who's in the back, well ... you're going to feel a whole lot better!'

* * *

From a traffic patrol PC's pocket book concerning a motorist who had committed several motoring offences:
Description: Long blond curly hair – effeminate.
Occupation: Male stripper.
Statement: 'Well, dearie, I'm ever so sorry and all that, but I've just had a nose-bleed and my big-ends have gone.'

* * *

Traffic patrol PC to somewhat dubious witness to an accident, 'Are you really *sure* you *saw* this accident?'

Witness, after thinking carefully for a moment, 'Well ... I suppose you could say I more or less heard it out of the corner of my eye.'

CID

From Dick Kirby of the Sweeney

All murders are awful but the one which I helped to investigate late in 1979 was particularly dreadful.

The victim was a 32-year-old East End housewife who had been stabbed to death in her own home. No motive for the killing was present – no sexual molestation, no robbery. Research into the background of the victim revealed her private life to be above reproach. In short, she had been a very nice person who lived happily with her husband in a very pleasant house.

All of us in the murder squad were outraged by the murder. She could easily have been our wife, girlfriend or daughter. For no reason at all, she had been literally slashed to death in the hallway of her own home. The offence was what is known in police parlance as a 'sticker'. That is, where there are no obvious suspects. Therefore, very soon the tried and trusted pattern of murder investigation emerged – just plain slog and plenty of it.

As 1979 passed in 1980, we were no further forward in achieving a result. One of my tasks was house-to-house investigation, starting from the murder scene and radiating into an ever-increasing area. One of the people I had to interview had begun to irritate me. Mr Sidney Bartholomew worked for the post office, and appointment after appointment was broken, due to the fact that he, like us, worked unsocial hours. Not his fault, of course, but it wasn't getting the job done.

Eventually – happy day! I managed to make a firm appointment with the elusive Sidney. Clutching my clipboard and a sheaf of questionnaires, I knocked on Mr Bartholomew's front door for the umpteenth time. That gentleman finally opened the door and, introducing myself, I stepped into the hallway.

'Morning!' I said briskly, anxious to get down to the inquiry. 'Where shall we go – in here?' I pointed to the lounge.

'No, not in there,' replied Mr Bartholomew. 'I haven't finished decorating it yet. Come into the back room.'

On entering the back room, I sat down, clipped a questionnaire onto the clipboard and pulled out my pen.

'Well, Mr Bartholomew, I take it you know what all this is about?'

'Yes,' he replied. There was a few seconds' pause and then he continued, 'My wife isn't impressed with this at all, you know.'

I looked up angrily. For me this was the final straw and I could feel my temper rising. 'Say that again,' I demanded.

'My – er, wife,' he stammered. 'She's not very impressed with it.'

'Is that right?' I asked in as quiet a voice as I could muster.

Mr Bartholomew appeared unwilling to meet my gaze, as well he might. 'Er ... yes ... yes, it is.'

I have been told that when I become really annoyed my voice drops almost to a whisper before rising to a crescendo. 'Well!' I whispered. 'Now isn't that just too f.....g bad!' Sidney Bartholomew said nothing but looked intently at his feet. Warming to my task, I continued, 'Let me tell you something, shall I, pal? We've interviewed three thousand people on this inquiry and, if necessary, we'll interview three thousand more. We haven't got a result yet but we're not going to give up. We're slogging our guts out thirteen hours a day. Do you know the last time I had a day off? Well do you?'

'Er ... no, no. I'm afraid I don't,' replied the now nervous Sidney as he fixed his eyes ever firmer on the carpet.

'Well, for your information squire, I can't f.....g remember so I can't f.....g tell you! That's how long it is! For weeks I've been asking what seems millions of people the same f.....g questions to get a result. Now I'll tell you something, my old son. I'm absolutely mortified that your missus isn't too impressed with the way things have been going. But give her my compliments will you and tell her from me that no matter *how* dissatisfied she is, we are going to carry on until we get a result – whether *she's* impressed or not. NOW IS THAT CLEAR?'

'Yes, sir,' replied the crimson Sidney. 'It is sir,' he nodded dutifully. There was a moment's pause before Mr Bartholomew cleared his throat. 'You see ...' he began nervously. 'What my wife isn't impressed with ... is the fact that I haven't finished decorating the front room.'

* * *

During an interview with a dirty, fat, scruffy, untidy, long fair-haired local villain, the detective sergeant began the session by saying, 'I would think you're definitely in the frame for this one, Fatty, my old son. The witness saw you very clearly and says that the person responsible was dirty, fat and scruffy with long, untidy, fair hair. What've you to say about that?'

'Well, Sarge,' began Fatty, rubbing his greasy chin thoughtfully. 'I would say I was well built, clean, smart, wiv' short red hair. Or at least I will be by the time this gits ter court.'

Actually, it was during the course of this burglary investigation that the CID searched Fatty's house. During the search Fatty's sister suddenly appeared.

'Hallo,' said the detective sergeant. 'What's your name then?'

Fatty's legal mind snapped quickly into action. 'Don't tell 'im nuffink, Kathy.'

* * *

Detective sergeant Rawlingshaw was very conscious of his weight and was regularly on diets. In spite of weighing in at around sixteen stone he assured himself and anyone who was daft enough to listen that he was just 'big boned'. It was whilst he was investigating a drive-out petrol theft that the light finally dawned.

'What did he look like, this bloke?' the sergeant asked the attendant.

'Very big,' she replied.

'Big? What do you mean "big"?'

'All right *fat*, then,' said the girl.

'How fat?'

'Well nowhere near as fat as you,' came the honest but crushing response.

* * *

Detective Sergeant George Wilson to the informant of a long-running office theft: 'So how often do you collect this money, Mr Byrne?'

'Once a month every Wednesday, sur.'

* * *

Even at busy stations 3.30 am can be a fairly dormant period and it is at times like this that an emergency call can receive far more police attention than it would otherwise merit.

Take 'a woman screaming at 58 Odell Street', for instance. A woman screaming is certainly dramatic, it could be anything from a nightmare to a murder. But this 'woman screaming' was caused not by a phantom rapist or a mysterious intruder but by a two-and-a-half-inch grey mouse that was scuttling cheerfully around her bedroom. Her husband was as petrified as she was and it was not until the arrival of the constabulary that her fears were at all eased. The heavy police presence did rather smack of overkill, consisting as it did of two panda cars, one area-car, five male hunters and one blonde huntress. However, in spite of moving every chair, carpet, cupboard and curtain, not a trace of the creature could be found in the room. He had escaped, it was believed, via the partially opened window.

It was whilst sitting in the kitchen supping the grateful couple's tea that their pleasantries were interrupted by the communications officer from the station. 'Units at 58 Odell Street,' he called, 'what's the latest update on your "woman screaming"? Over.'

The blonde huntress was the first to pick up a personal radio. 'I'm afraid the "suspect" escaped from a window on the arrival of police. Over.'

It was at that moment that a sixteen-stone detective sergeant strolled into the front office at the station and heard the end of the transmission. 'Where's the location of that call?' he snapped.

'58 Odell Street,' replied the communications officer. 'But all it is ...' His attempt at an explanation fell on deaf ears; the burly detective was already panting towards his Ford.

It was the screech of brakes that alerted the chatting constables. As three of them jockeyed for a view from the kitchen window, the detective sergeant leaped from his car and raced through the open front door. 'What the bloody hell's going on here?' he demanded. 'No wonder your suspect's escaped!'

'Actually he hasn't,' said the area-car driver as he glanced down behind the gas-stove. He stooped, then held up a sprung mousetrap with a still warm corpse attached. 'Here y'are, Sarge,' he announced gravely. 'Load of grief this one, bound to make the *Guardian* ... dies whilst being arrested.'

* * *

The elderly gipsy prisoner's statement was taken down by the detective sergeant but when asked to sign it, it was discovered that the old reprobate could neither read nor write.

After the necessary 'cross' was made, the detective thought a little footnote should be added to explain the prisoner's lack of academic ability. This he did on the very next line by pointing out that the prisoner was an 'ilitereat gypsey'.

* * *

Two detectives were doing a surveillance in Dulwich Park after a series of indecent assaults. They had separated and one of them soon saw what he thought was a Frenchman carrying a handbag and wearing just a hip-length shirt and the briefest of 'G' strings. Thinking this was his man, the detective followed him through the woods. Suddenly the suspect disappeared. A few moments later the detective heard a noise behind him and turned to see the suspect confronting him minus his 'G' string.

He is still trying to live down running for help.

* * *

Detective Derek Sharman showed all his experience in one clever hunch. Whilst on the telephone to another police station he was heard to say, 'The villain's name is Frenchie.' He then paused and added in a quiet confidential manner, 'I think that could well be a nickname, though.'

* * *

Derek again: 'He was lying in a vertical position, Your Worship.'

* * *

A Croydon detective inspector, after grilling a suspect, turned to junior members of his department and thoughtfully announced, 'This bloke is either telling the truth, or he's f.....g lying.'

* * *

The non-smoker Liverpool detective had spent some time interviewing a prisoner about a series of arson attacks. He eventually broke off the interview to ask the station officer, 'Could my prisoner have a light, Sarge?'

* * *

Tom O'Reardon, although extremely likeable, was not the brightest detective in the metropolitan police and many of his remarks found their way into station folklore. He was at his bewildering best when trying to be helpful and never more so than when, one Tuesday afternoon, the detective inspector entered the CID office to study the various transport timetables.

It seemed that the D.I. had five of a six-man robbery team in custody. They were due in court the following morning and he had just been delighted to discover that the sixth member had been arrested in Dundee. It would obviously save an enormous amount of time and money if the whole gang could now be tried together. The problem, therefore, was how does one travel from London to Dundee, collect a prisoner and return in time for a 10.30am court the following morning?

The railway almanacs were perused at great length and many phone calls made but still the schedule was too tight. Finally someone suggested a plane. Now because of the expense, this form of conveying prisoners is usually frowned upon. Time, however, was running out and if Wally Swain, wheel-man extraordinaire, was to appear at Bow Street the following morning, then a plane would seem a necessity.

'The only problem I can see now,' said the D.I. to the assembled throng, 'is – is there an airport anywhere near there? Because we're going to look right berks if there's not.' He stared hopefully around the office but every face was blank.

Then to everyone's surprise, Tom cleared his throat and was obviously about to speak. The D.I. looked up expectantly, 'Well, Tom, is there? Do you really know if there's an airport in Dundee?'

'I don't know about an airport, sir,' said Tom helpfully. 'But I think there's a marmalade factory.'

* * *

Detective Sergeant Barry Whetstone and Detective Sergeant Archie Caldwell were considered to be the academics of their department. They had been engaged in a long drawn out and complicated fraud case. 'A real brain-hurting job,' as they frequently told their less intellectual colleagues.

One morning, in the canteen at Scotland Yard, the pair decided to 'spoof' for the coffees. Spoofing is a widespread force tradition in which a group of any number can gamble as to who will pay for the drinks. Each person can hold from nought to three coins in a closed hand and then must simply guess the collective total of coins. Those who guess correctly drop out; the last person pays.

Barry Whetstone, who held two coins, decided his friend held none and therefore called 'two'. Archie, after great deliberations, called 'five'. The two intellectual wizards then opened their hands. Barry held two coins, Archie held none.

'But why did you call five when you held none?' asked the puzzled Barry.

'I put the wrong hand on the table,' mumbled the other academic.

* * *

Officious CID officer lecturing recruits during their first week of service: 'You can prevent crime all day long – but that won't stop them doing it.'

Same CID officer, once more trying to impress with his local knowledge, 'Of course, that one's a raving poufta. I've been dealing with him for years.'

* * *

Detective Sergeant Martin Jewell had arrested a GPO employee and was enjoying an amiable conversation in the CID car on the way to the station. 'Now take Abraham Lincoln for example ...' began Martin.

'What post office does he work in?' asked the inquisitive prisoner.

* * *

Criminal Record form description. *'Type of personality: Unhappy.'*
Being arrested may have had something to do with it.

* * *

A certain London detective prided himself on his image. He, at least,
considered he was a well-turned out, smooth, sympathetic operator.

Not so everyone.

An official complaint about him was made by a prisoner who,
unfortunately, did not know his name.

'Can you describe this officer then?' asked the investigating inspector.

'Oh yeah,' agreed the complainant. 'You can't miss him. He looks
like Columbo with his dirty rotten raincoat and his wonky eye – and he
gets right on yer tits when he tries to be a father figure.'

* * *

Sergeant Dan Oliver was given a new young crime squad to blood. He
decided to take them out to teach them the rudiments of surveillance.
With apparent good fortune, they soon picked up 'Elusive Eric',
probably the biggest 'dip' (pickpocket) on the manor.

'Play it canny, lads,' instructed Dan. 'Eric will either start dipping or
meet his cronies. Whichever way, you'll learn something.'

The surveillance worked a treat. They followed Eric for more than a
mile and he never once suspected they were there. He led them in fact
to one of the biggest haunts of cut-throats and thieves in South London
– Camberwell magistrates' court.

* * *

One problem with police-criminal slang, is that not all criminals are
conversant with it. Yet many young policemen feel that immediately
they make the rank of detective they should scatter their conversation
with certain words and expressions. For instance, few detectives
nowadays will finish a conversation with 'Cheerio', 'Ta-ta', or even

123

'Nice to have seen you'. Instead, it will be the over-used television detective request to 'Give me a bell sometime, eh?' Likewise they will never search a prisoner's home address; instead, they will 'spin his drum'. And of course nowadays no one ever lies; instead, they tell 'porkies'. Many bright young detectives who would experience difficulty in finding a bad smell take great pains to learn these expressions, not always with the happiest of results.

Take the rather superior young detective who was interviewing a Camberwell burglar. 'So, what made you pick that particular drum then, sunshine?'

The suspect looked totally confused for a full half-minute before replying, 'Nah, it weren't no "drum", guv, was it? It was a bleedin' video ... wasn't it?'

* * *

Few people are more boring – particularly to non-smokers – than those who, once a month, announce their intention to 'pack it up for good'. What will happen is what always happens. The symbolic last packet will be opened with great reverence and friends and colleagues will be made painfully aware they are in the presence of a martyr.

Derek Haslam from Addington police station tells of one such addict who was preparing for his ninth abstention. Fed up with his previous attempts, the colleagues of this nicotine-starved detective decided to assist him in his efforts. This they did by the insertion of an exploding capsule in one of his filtertips. This prank had been made easy by the smoker's habit of leaving his current packet open on his desk.

As the morning passed, eager heads raised each time a deep soothing puff was taken. By lunch time the contents of the packed had halved. Still no explosion delighted the watchers. The attention of the observers was finally distracted by the arrival of a uniformed inspector who announced that the owner of a warehouse not a million miles from the station was in the waiting room and demanding to see a detective. It appeared that this gentleman had just suffered his fourth break-in in as many weeks and he wished to discover just what the CID planned to do about it. 'He's not very happy,' added the inspector needlessly.

'Don't worry, guv,' assured our smoker, who had a reputation as something of a smoothie, 'I'll sweeten him up for you.' So saying, he rose from his typewriter, picked up his fags and left on his task of appeasement. The raised voice from the waiting room soon gave way to more moderate tones. Eventually even a chuckle was heard.

No one actually *heard* the cigarette being offered, of course, but everyone heard it explode. I mean, if there is just one exploding cigarette in a pack of twenty, well it's a dead cert who is going to get it, isn't it?

I think it's called Sod's law.

* * *

Detective Constables Wimbourne and Binn travelled from London to Scotland by plane to pick up a prisoner. It was arranged with the Scottish police that both they and the prisoner would be ready and waiting. The intrepid detectives could then catch the next plane back, which happened to be the last one of the day and also the very plane on which they had flown to Scotland.

As the plane landed, they asked the hostess to save them three rear seats, then ran out into the airport building. The handover went very smoothly and the paperwork took only minutes. Soon the detectives and the villain were climbing back up the steps of the plane into the specially requested three rear seats.

A period of time elapsed and they began to realise they were the only occupants of the aircraft. (They *are* detectives, you see.) A little later they also realised there were no lights on the plane. (They are also very *bright* detectives.) Even later they realised they were on the *wrong* plane!

Falling down the steps, the three figures dashed across the airfield waving furiously – just as the only other aircraft in sight took off ... for London.

* * *

Detective Sergeant Fred Parrish had a great sense of humour, which was just as well because there were times in the Serious Crime Squad when it was really needed. Particularly during long and boring observations.

Take the observation in a busy North London shopping centre, for example. Fred and another member of the squad were tucked up in the rear of an 'observation' van. They were concealed in the locked goods section and the van therefore appeared unattended. At least that was what the traffic warden thought as she wrote out her ticket. She had no problems until she went to place it under the wipers. As she reached forward a jet of water hit the screen and both wipers swung quickly into operation. She jumped back and they promptly stopped. She then made another attempt – with the same result.

Walking stealthily round to the other side of the vehicle, she peeped gingerly into the empty cabin – and the horn gave a long angry blast. Biting her lip, she spent several minutes deep in thought before summoning up her courage for another attempt. This time, as she leaned carefully forward – the engine started.

Folding her book, she walked away.

Community Coppering

Johnny Sommers, a community copper from Greater Manchester, recalls asking a young teenage girl about her school's impending trip to Paris.

'You're a lucky girl, Sharon,' said John enviously. 'I wish I was going. I suppose this time next week you'll be walking down the Champs-Elysées or Montmartre?'

'Nah,' sniffed the unimpressed girl. 'I can't stand all them stuffy museums meself. I'm just goin' to sit on the beach.'

* * *

PC Keith Rose was asked to judge a fancy-dress parade at one of his local primary schools. Although the general standard was high, there was still one lad that stood out from the rest. His beautiful 15th-century costume showed an amazing attention to detail. What puzzled Keith, however, was the dog that the boy led with such exaggerated deliberation. It was obvious by the pose that the animal was an essential part of the character portrayed. Unfortunately, the lad carried no clue as to his identity. Because such effort had gone into the outfit, Keith was at first reluctant to spoil the illusion by asking the youngster just who he was supposed to be.

At last, feeling he had no choice, Keith approached the boy. 'Marvellous costume, David, really great!' he enthused. 'Er – exactly who are you?' he added, still eyeing the dog.

'Dick Whittington,' responded the child proudly.

'Oh, I see!' replied Keith, not really seeing at all. 'Dick Whittington, eh?'

'That's right,' said David proudly. 'Dick Whittington and his dog.'

'But – er, I thought Dick Whittington actually had a cat?'

129

'Oh, yeah, he did,' explained the boy cheerfully. 'But we ain't got a cat so I fort I'd use me dog.'

* * *

From Cliff Morgan

I was on duty in Cwmbran New Town when I received a call from a local woman who was estranged from her husband. The family were well known to police for a number of reasons, not the least being her husband's frequent suicide attempts. (Including one where he deliberately drove his car flat out into a motorway bridge but climbed out of the wreckage unmarked.)

The lady had apparently returned to her home to find the doors locked from within. She rightly suspected that her husband was inside, making yet another attempt to end his life. I attended and tried all doors and windows but without success. I notified the station and an elderly sergeant (thank goodness now retired) and a rather ineffectual recruit (very soon to depart to become a kitchen salesman – also thank goodness) arrived to back me up. I effected an entry – well, to be precise I kicked in the front door – and found the scenario that every policeman dreads. There, lying on the floor, with his head resting at a neck-breaking angle on the edge of a chair, was the estranged husband. An empty bottle lay on the table and an open suicide note was propped nearby.

I was surprised how quickly my first aid training came to the fore. I picked up the nearest wrist; it was pulseless, ice cold and a horrible shade of white: I then glanced up at the sergeant and gave a subtle, almost imperceptible shake of the head. The sergeant, with the finesse of a Borgia, cheerily announced, 'Oh well, he's gone, luv.'

For a moment I could have sworn I detected the briefest of smiles on her face.

Because there was nothing further I could do for the deceased, I decided to spend a minute or two reassuring the recruit, who, after all, had never seen a corpse before. It was then, as I finished pointing out all the obvious signs of death, that the corpse groaned and shifted to a more comfortable position. In my haste to pronounce him dead I had taken the pulse from the arm that he had been lying on for the past two hours. The circulation in that particular limb had stopped completely. An ambulance was summoned (and the undertaker cancelled) and the husband swifted away to hospital, to live – at least between suicide attempts – happily ever after.

To be fair, the wife did show genuine distress. 'Trust the bastard not to do anything properly,' she sobbed.

* * *

PC George Carling was left in a South London flat which had been the scene of a serious shooting. His instructions were to admit no one until photographs and forensic tests had been made. After a short time the victim's friends arrived to take some of her clothing to the hospital. George of course refused them entry and they soon left – after carefully locking the door from the outside, with poor George, somewhat embarrassed, inside.

* * *

From PC Steven Morgan of Lincoln
An eighty-two-year-old lady named Sarah finally left her husband after sixty years of marriage, twelve kids and something like three million grandchildren; she claimed she had never been so happy. All went well for a week or so, until the old man discovered her whereabouts. He turned up at the old people's sheltered home where she was staying and called for the police.

I arrived and he told me that he was determined she should return with him. I explained that it was a decision she would need to make herself and there must be no compulsion. Sarah, however, wasn't having any of it and simply refused to see him or discuss it with him. All of this conversation had taken place through the closed door of the old lady's bedsit. Eventually the staff decided that the disturbance had gone on for long enough and requested the old fellow to leave. He reluctantly, and very angrily, began to withdraw.

Suddenly being struck by a last compelling argument, he requested a final minute at Sarah's door.

'All right,' agreed the warden, 'but make it quick.'

The old chap limped back to the flat and banged once with his walking stick. 'Sarah! Are you there?' he demanded.

'Yes,' came the guarded and muffled reply.

'Well, Sarah ... you can bury your f.....g self!'

* * *

A very senior officer who was rash enough to be found walking the streets was approached by a puzzled American tourist.

'Excuse me, sir,' began the American politely. 'I'm visiting your historical town of Greenwich, England. Could you kindly direct me to the birthplace of General the Duke of Nelson?'

The commander of 'R' division drew himself up stiffly. 'Actually, Nelson was born in Suffolk.'

'I see, sir,' said the tourist thoughtfully. 'And how many blocks away is that?'

* * *

During the serious Tottenham riots of October 1985, there were times when parts of the Broadwater Farm estate must have seemed like hell itself. With the murder of Keith Blakelock, the shooting of Stuart Patt, and the enormous number of injuries sustained by the remainder of the police, 'The Farm' was not a good place to be.

By 3.30am though, parts of the area had quietened enough for many of the PCs to at least sit down. This they did on whatever happened to be handy. Low walls, kerbstones and milk-crates, all were used. Buildings and overturned cars, however, continued to smoulder. Everywhere was broken glass and the acrid smell of smoke. Amidst the weak and often contrasting orders that came from the senior officer on the scene, there was one rule that was consistently enforced. No member of the public could either enter or leave the estate.

Suddenly a small family saloon made to turn into one of the small entrances. It was instantly stopped by a smoke-blackened copper who stepped out in front with a raised arm. The dumb-struck Asian driver wound down his window and stared in astonishment at the devastation all around.

'Whatever is going on?' he exclaimed.

'Don't worry, mate,' called a weary copper from an upturned milk-crate. 'It's only community policing.'

* * *

From George Wilcoxon, South London PC

In 1983 a by-election took place in North Southwark that became known as 'the Tatchell election'. Because of the interest of the media, this drew several strange and even downright barmy candidates – sixteen in number.

As a result of this, most polling stations had a small army of helpers and canvassers milling around just outside their front doors. These ladies and gentlemen would be all eager to provide, in support of their own candidate of course, any help a constituent might need in order to vote. Our local Catholic school, for instance, had nine such helpers, all of whom huddled together in a small doorway away from the incessant rain. Strictly speaking, these canvassers should not have been in the building at all but the tolerant presiding officer was prepared to grant them at least temporary shelter away from the elements. My own function, as the attendant policeman, was simply to follow the instructions of the presiding officer inside the building and ensure there were no breaches of the peace outside.

Everything had been fairly uneventful until the arrival of a blind, arthritic old lady in a wheelchair. Her elderly companion, who was pushing the 'chair', appeared only marginally healthier herself. It would be difficult to imagine anything more likely to galvanise the emotions of the party faithful than this pair.

'Don't you worry, luv', 'Here, I'll hold the door', 'This way, dear'. Each of the supporters became the epitome of their sycophantic masters. Eventually, and in spite of the abundance of help, the elderly pair entered the room where the votes were to be cast, with their retinue of determined helpers trailing behind. The seated lady announced her name and address with great confidence and, on receiving her voting paper from the presiding officer, grasped it firmly between her gnarled fingers. Her companion, on receiving her own slip, then turned the chair towards the voting cubicles. It was at this stage that the problems began.

'We'll push you into the cubicle so you can reach the shelf from your chair,' said one party worker.

'Yes, good idea,' chorused the others quickly, each secretly furious they had not thought of the idea first. Unfortunately, the width of the cubicle was two inches less than the width of the wheelchair. In spite of much wiggling, this fact could not be altered.

'We'll have to give you your voting slip on your lap,' said the Socialist Workers' Party lady.

This was all very well, until the voter went to make her cross, when the thick and usually sharp pencil that was secured to the side of the cubicle by string went straight through the paper. I pointed out her predicament to the presiding officer and suggested that the placing of a book underneath the slip would suffice for her to make her cross. The old girl, however, was of independent character and asked if the cubicles were of the same design that they had been when she had been sighted. Reassured they had not changed since Disraeli, she said she would hold the paper against the batten that ran down the side of the cubicle. This proved too narrow.

'The desk!' called the presiding officer. 'Here, try it on my desk.' To emphasise his point he began to clear a space on the cluttered table-top. The enthusiastic band of helpers then turned the wheelchair in his direction and began to push it the few short yards. Unfortunately the old lady was still in determined possession of the officially authorised heavy pencil. This pencil was in turn still attached to the piece of string. The string, of course, was attached to the cubicle.

'Look out!' I yelled as the entire section of cubicles, some six in number, began to twist and swing ominously. Feeling some unexpected resistance to her tightly clutched pencil, the blind lady gave the cord an extra and irritable tug. The entire section of cubicles groaned and creaked for about two seconds – before crashing impressively to the floor.

At first I thought the whole episode made out an unanswerable case for these pencils to be attached by elastic. Then on reflection I imagined the horror and possible decapitations that could result as the thing catapulted back out of her hand.

Once the cross was made, the merry band of helpers rapidly disappeared, obviously believing there was nothing more to gain from already cast votes. The two old ladies, meanwhile, were determined to prove they were not a spent force. This they did by running over the foot of the school caretaker who was vainly attempting to right the capsized cubicles. I had by that time acquired the feeling that these two old dears could well be twin disaster areas. It was this assumption, rather than any particular gallantry, that caused me to escort them politely from the premises.

Great confusion was caused by the large number of candidates in this election. No one was more confused than the elderly lady who accompanied her husband to vote. They went to the desk, where the presiding officer asked them their names and addresses. On receiving their ballot papers they went into adjoining cubicles where, presumably, the husband swiftly made his cross. He returned across the hall and dropped his vote into the large metal ballot-box. The wife, meanwhile, stood deliberating with the marking pencil poised thoughtfully in her mouth. On two or three occasions, she looked questioningly back at her husband, then resumed her study of the paper. This routine went on for some time with the husband showing signs of increasing irritation. Finally, she turned once more towards him and called in a plaintive tone, 'George, oo did yer say?'

George seemed about to explode. 'O'Grady, yer silly cow – O'Grady!'

'He ain't on the list, George.'

'O'course 'e is, yer daft cow!' So saying, he strode the few yards across to her and, seizing her hand, banged it down twice onto the paper in the shape of a cross. He then thrust the paper into her hand and told her to 'Stuff it in the bleedin' box.'

'Ah,' said the presiding officer as the couple left the hall. 'A suffragette, no doubt!'

* * *

The large, nineteen-feet-high load was driven by the driver down a route he had never taken before and he had become well and truly stuck under an eighteen-feet-high railway bridge. The home beat officer had received the call on his personal radio and, turning the corner, asked the policeman's perennial question: 'What's all this about, then?'

'Well,' said the frustrated driver. 'You see, I got this low bridge to deliver and I've lost me way ...'

* * *

From Alan Harston

PC John Waters from Clapham is one of nature's better people. With a mentally handicapped child of his own, he is very much into all aspects of voluntary work that relate to mental welfare. These range from fund-raising to using his annual leave to take other people's handicapped children on holiday.

Just before Christmas 1980, he was asked by a couple of schools on his patch if he would be Father Christmas in their yule-tide festivities. True to fashion, John accepted the part and, with his usual conviction, 'borrowed' the appropriate outfit – beard, cloak, boots, whiskers and bulbous nose.

Sadly, a few of the children were ill, so John decided to visit them at home to deliver their presents. One of the youngsters lived in a high-rise block surrounded by muddy, patchy grass and a network of paths and walls. John remained dressed in his gear which caused no little amusement to a gang of three teenage tearaways who were hanging around the entrance to the block. Father Christmas, therefore, not only received a torrent of abuse going in but even more coming out.

The foul-mouthed yobs, however, overlooked two quite important points, the first being that John knew each of them very well indeed (and if he had been apparent to them in his usual blue, instead of red and white, they would have known him) and the second being that, all-round good egg though he was, he was not a soft touch for anyone. By the time he had drawn alongside them for the second time, he had taken enough of their abuse. Seizing the opportunity to take revenge in a way that would not usually be allowed, he gave the biggest and loudest of the three a good firm dig. The chosen yob was sitting with his legs dangling from a wall that separated the path from an extremely muddy, grassed area. A second later he was spreadeagled in the mud looking pleadingly up at Father Christmas who, bending forward over the wall, gave the following helpful advice.

'Now go down to the nick and tell 'em that Father Christmas thumped you.'

* * *

A home beat officer went into a Camberwell school after being requested to give a talk to the infants on uniforms. Having drawn appreciative gasps from the children by quickly yanking off his clip-on tie, he asked the assembled children, 'And why do you think I wear a tie like this?'

At first there was no response.

'Oh come on, now,' said the officer, warming to his task. 'Someone must know, surely?'

One little five-year-old boy shyly raised his hand.

'Yes? Why do you think I can take my tie off so quickly, young man?'

'So you can jump into bed quicker, sir?'

Out of the mouths of babes and sucklings ...

* * *

From ex-PC Peter Gurney
I was patrolling a residential beat late one night in Babbacombe when I saw a rather powerfully built fellow pushing a 500 twin motorcycle. I stopped him to check he was in lawful possession and found he had been pushing it for the last four miles and was almost home. He told me he was on his way to work at a bakery twenty miles away in Exeter and the bike had spluttered to a standstill some ten minutes into his journey. He had spent an hour trying to repair it but had finally given up and, after telephoning his employer from a call-box, decided to push the

machine home. He lived about three hundred yards away at the top of a steep hill and, because he appeared on the verge of exhaustion, I assisted him to push it up the one-in-six slope.

It took us some fifteen minutes to reach his house only to find that his wife had locked up for the night and his key would not turn in the lock. I thought I had done about all that I could do and bade him goodnight. I left him calling loudly through the letter box.

I took a narrow footpath that ran alongside his house into a neighbouring street. As I passed by his rear garden, I heard the sound of a window opening. Peering through the gloom I could just make out the shape of an apparently nude female assisting a rather short tubby man to descend from a first-floor back window. The man suddenly slipped and, giving a muffled cry, crashed some nine or ten feet onto the rear patio. I did not need to be the greatest detective in the world to realise what had happened. As the window slid closed, the man limped swiftly towards the rear gate and for the second time in as many minutes received a nasty shock – this time when he saw me. The drop from the window had done him no good at all. His trousers were badly torn, as was his right leg and his bottom lip. His total dress consisted of the aforementioned trousers, a shirt and a right sock. In his hand he carried his shoes, a sweater and a rather gaudily patterned pair of underpants.

'Bloody hell, guv'nor!' he panted, clutching both shoes against his heart. 'You scared the shits out'a me!'

'Don't let me worry you,' I assured him. 'I'm the least of your problems. That bloke's about twice the size of Samson. If I was you I'd put as much distance between you and him as soon as possible before he finds out exactly where you've been.'

He nodded agreement. 'I'll just finish dressing and I'll be off.' He quickly pulled on the sweater and slipped the underpants into a trouser pocket. Then bending down, he put on his right shoe. He was just about to ease into his left one, when he suddenly realised he had no left sock. 'Oh my God!' he exclaimed. 'Isn't that terrible?'

'What is it?' I asked, thinking he could take a pick from any of a half-dozen mishaps that had just befallen him.

'No left sock!'

'Well, I would hardly think it's your greatest disaster,' I observed acidly.

'Oh it is! It is!' he insisted. 'I mean ...' He looked around as if

138

searching for words. ' ... A bloke ain't got no dignity with only one sock.'

* * *

During the visit of Princess Anne to a Camberwell school, all the local home beat officers were posted to security points. One of them was designated as a 'spotter'.

'What the hell does a "spotter" do, Sarge?' he understandably asked.

'Well,' said the sergeant, who knew even less than the PC about the required functions of spotters. 'I suppose you just patrol the area in general and, er ... just try to spot something unusual ... wouldn't you say?'

The perplexed constable then rashly stated that nothing ever happened in Camberwell. A few minutes later, still complaining, he went out on his patrol ... just in time to see a Chinaman step off a moving bus straight through the windscreen of a following car!

'Congratulations!' said the straight-faced sergeant. 'Extremely well done. To observe a Chinaman step through the windscreen of a moving car must be spotting of the very highest order! Here,' he added with a knowing sly wink, 'you've practised, haven't you?'

* * *

From Peter Hotchkiss, Thames Valley

When I first joined the police force I was astonished at the number of marital disputes I was called upon to deal with. I remember dealing with one particular family as many as three times a week. What stuck in my mind most was the way they would persistently interrupt each other and make it impossible to hear what each was saying. There would be an endless babble of differing sound, from the time I arrived until the time that I left.

On something like my fifteenth visit to the flat I was surprised to find the call had not been made as a result of the usual domestic punch-up but as a result of the wife being accosted by a flasher on her way home from work. During her recounting of the incident, the husband remained impassive and silent behind his newspaper. I asked for as many details as she could remember about the suspect and she gave a fairly comprehensive description. I remember revelling in the unusual luxury of having to listen to just one voice.

As an afterthought I asked her if the flasher had spoken to her at all. 'As a matter of fact he did.'

I waited for a moment but no further dialogue was forthcoming. 'And what did he say?' I persisted.

She pulled herself up erect and glanced haughtily towards her husband who still showed total indifference.

Raising her voice an octave, she announced in ringing tones, 'He said I had a lovely pair of tits.'

Peering momentarily over the top of his paper, the husband made his first utterance since my arrival. 'How did he know?' he asked quietly. 'Did he prod 'em with his white stick?'

* * *

From Alan Weatherall, Greater Manchester

I was patrolling a large housing estate where there had been a great deal of daytime theft and vandalism. I soon noticed that John Shadbolt, an incorrigible eleven-year-old thief, one-boy demolition squad and persistent truant, appeared rather anxious to avoid meeting me. Striding out briskly, I circuited a couple of blocks and he almost ran into me on a corner.

'Why aren't you at school, John?' I asked, which was my customary opening to any conversation with this boy.

'I'm ill, sir,' he replied. Which, as an answer, was even more customary than my question.

'You look all right to me – who said you were ill?'

'The doctor did, sir.'

'Oh yeah, he did, did he?' I then adopted my superior knowing tone. 'And just what did he say was wrong with you?'

Johnny's beady little eyes lit up triumphantly. 'He said I 'ad verbal diarrhoea, sir!'

Women Police

The hierarchy of the police has, on many occasions, unsuccessfully tried to implement the twenty-four-hour clock as standard practice throughout the force. This practice has been reasonably easy for those of us who have been members of Her Majesty's forces. However, as the following dialogue shows, it has not been so easily assimilated by youngsters who were never as much as Brownies or Cubs.

Vastly experienced and world-weary Manchester detective sergeant, to a very young WPC: 'Young lady, you have entered a crime in the book and you have timed the offence as "twenty-five hundred hours". As there are sadly only twenty-four hours in any one day, could you give me some little clue as to when this offence may have taken place?'

The embarrassed and rosy-cheeked young girl screwed up her face in deep concentration for a moment, then helpfully replied, 'I'm afraid I really don't know, Sergeant ... is it tomorrow?'

* * *

Ill winds prevail throughout all police stations, as the young Motherwell WPC discovered during her first week of night duty. She had arrested a drunk who gained his revenge by urinating over her legs. She stood with her prisoner in the charge-room together with her soaked stockings and saturated footwear.

The harassed station officer entered – and promptly congratulated her on her shiny shoes!

* * *

143

The young Brixton WPC had made her first arrest and was then lumbered with the paperwork. 'It's this CRO form, Sarge,' she muttered worriedly. 'I don't know what I need to insert in the "Marks and peculiarities" section.'

'Don't worry, gel,' the sergeant assured her. 'You can shove down just about anything that's not covered by the rest of the form.'

'Such as?'

The sergeant sighed deeply. 'Have a chat with him. Ask him about any operation scars and suchlike. You know the sort of thing. Anything he tells you ... well, bung it down, for Gawd's sake.'

The completed form seemed to indicate that her questioning of the prisoner was thorough indeed. Under 'Marks and peculiarities' was inserted: *'Minus left testicle, scar in centre of forehead.'*

* * *

WPC Joanne Busutow was filling in the 'Vehicle Description' form and asked the victim of a car theft, 'Did you have any badges on the car, sir?'

'Only one,' came the reply.

'And that was?'

'"Be a good neighbour".'

* * *

An extremely unfortunate man was lying underneath a bus in the Walworth Road and suffering from all the injuries that one tends to sustain when one is knocked flat by a bus – mangled arms, legs, and collar-bone, for instance. As he lay there trapped and desperately listening for the ambulance and fire-brigade heavy rescue team, an extremely pretty, if somewhat naive, young WPC arrived. She took off her hat and wriggled underneath the bus to lie alongside him. His confidence evaporated, however, when she whispered sweetly, 'Do you wish to go to hospital, sir?'

* * *

A Kensington inspector to a rather glamorous WPC: 'Can you drive me to Scotland Yard, Miss Taylor?'

'Not at this precise moment, sir,' said the preoccupied young lady. 'I've just broken my nail.'

* * *

The newly divorced WPC was suffering from the effects of putting up three shelves in her kitchen. After studying her hands at some length she thoughtfully announced, 'I was screwing so hard last night I've got blisters on my hands.'

* * *

David Beresford, a constable of some years' standing, was complaining about the encroachment of women police into the force. 'I've nothing against them, mind, but at times they outnumber us. We've already got six girls on our shift.'

'I know,' agreed WPC Marilyn Burns sympathetically. 'And even some of the blokes are a bit marginal.'

* * *

A rather heavy mature WPC at a North London station was in the habit of taking her holidays in obscure foreign parts, from where she fetched even more obscure foreign mementos.

'What mysterious creation do you think Liz will bring back this time?' asked the bright young WPC of a canteen group.

'Goat's testicles, probably,' said a facetious PC.

'Oh, that reminds me,' said the girl gratefully. 'I really must go to the doctor's ...'

*   *   *

WPC overheard in station canteen: 'I'm three weeks late. It's not that I'm paranoid about it – but I've had four pregnancy tests.'

Same WPC speaking of the person who was strongly fancied to be the cause of her apprehension. 'There are times when I could kill him. If he had a skirt on his big toe he'd fall in love with his bloody feet!'

*   *   *

WPC Jenny Harper answered a telephone query from the complaints bureau at Scotland Yard. 'You sound efficient,' said the caller. 'Are you a civilian?'

*   *   *

Every police station – I should think in the world – has its fair share of pleasantly potty callers. These individuals, who call as regular as clockwork, are kindly treated because, apart from being harmless, they often provide light relief. On the other hand, any station officer with a charge-room full of prisoners and a dozen of their irate relatives at the counter, is not necessarily enthusiastic when the local nutter walks in. At such times, the younger members of the relief will be introduced and assigned to a 'special task'. This task could be anything from Russian spies in the gas-cooker to – as ex-WPC Maureen Cooper discovered – dogs in a mincer.

'Don't ... you ... worry ... luv,' the station officer assured the caller, in the slow booming voice he reserved for halfwits and foreigners. 'This ... young ... lady ... policeman ... will ... sort ... it ... all ... out ... for ... you.' He turned to the new WPC and mouthed an aside. 'Just pop along to her flat and show the flag. She'll be quite happy then.'

'What's it all about, Sarge?' asked Maureen anxiously.

'She reckons the bloke upstairs kidnaps dogs and shoves 'em in a mincer. She'll be all right, though, once you've paid her a visit.' He turned once more to the caller. 'Off ... you ... go ... now ... Miss ... Murray. The lady ... policeman ... will ... follow ... you ... in ... a ... little ... while.'

Thirty minutes later the young recruit listened wide-eyed as the dastardly deeds of the upstairs lodger were related.

'And you say, Miss Murray, that he kidnaps these dogs and takes them downstairs into the cellar where he grinds them up in a mincer?'

'That's right, my dear,' agreed Miss Murray. 'In very small bits, he does.'

The girl then began a dutiful examination of the premises and instantly found a flaw in the allegation.

'But Miss Murray,' she said in bewilderment, 'you don't have a cellar.'

'I know, my dear!' exclaimed Miss Murray triumphantly. 'And that's the funny part about it.'

Sometimes, of course, these somewhat strange callers could be dealt with more easily at the station. Old Joe Buttle was such a case.

Joe would, according to ex-Sergeant Dan Butson, call in regularly because he was 'full of electricity' and could not sleep. At first Dan had no idea what to do, until an old copper took the caller into the waiting room and gave him a key.

'Now listen to me carefully, Joe boy,' he instructed. 'If you hold this key tight against this radiator for a while you will, what's called, "earth yourself". As soon as you've done that, you'll be able to go home and sleep like a log – got it?'

Joe was particularly keen to give this treatment a try and, sure enough, he emerged an hour later and told everyone he was now cured. The only problem was that whenever he couldn't sleep, regardless of the time of day or how busy the front counter happened to be, he would arrive cheerfully at the station where the sergeant would be expected to hand over the key post-haste. Trotting cheerfully into the waiting room, he would plug himself in for the best part of an hour before emerging with a serene smile. He would then return the key, thank everybody profusely and dash straight home to bed, where it was assumed he slept like a log.

The obvious problem with potty callers is that occasionally even they have genuine reasons for attending the station.

Take Elsie McNaughton, for example. The problem with Elsie was that there was no consistency in her complaints. One day it would be crocodiles, the next, spacemen. Therefore when she alleged three times in one day that her neighbours were trying to kill her – well, it wasn't exactly treated as the call of the year. Her insistency was finally rewarded by yet another WPC who visited her. 'Where'd you get all these shocks from, Elsie?' asked the girl, somewhat patronisingly.

'That wall there,' replied the worried Elsie.

The young WPC graciously placed her hand on the offending wall – and was promptly thrown halfway across the room by a voltage that almost took her arm off!

* * *

Six-feet-tall and extremely attractive Angela was being interviewed by the chief superintendent at the end of her probationary-constable period.

'Now you have finished your first two years,' he said, 'is there anything you're particularly keen on doing?'

'Well sir,' said the girl thoughtfully. 'I have always fancied being mounted.'

* * *

'I don't know why my car won't start, Sarge, I'm sure,' complained the exasperated Melinda as she arrived late for the third time in a week. 'The lads all said I should buy a can of "Dampstart" so I did and now it's even worse! I've soaked it for the last three mornings and it's worse than ever.'

'Let's have a look,' said the sergeant as he examined the offending can. 'You silly cow! It's windscreen cleaner!'

* * *

WPC Althea Tulloch applied for permission to move house. She smoothly filled in all the questions on the police administration forms until she arrived at the one which read, 'How can the premises be inspected?'

Being an extremely logical young lady she answered, 'By going there.' How else?

* * *

Glasgow WPC on being called to a suspicious fire: 'I think it's possibly a definite arson.'

* * *

WPC Jill Gains arrested a punk for carrying an offensive weapon – a knife. Shown under 'Marks and peculiarities' on the prisoner's description form were the words, *'Parrot perched on left shoulder.'*

'Why were you carrying the knife, son?' asked the station officer.

'I think it was to protect him from the parrot, Sarge,' cut in Jill helpfully.

* * *

Woman Police Sergeant Donna Kitchener tells the following. During a spate of terrorist activity a directive was issued to each station switchboard. It contained a list of questions to be asked should anyone telephone to announce they were about to make everyone in the building posthumous by blowing it up:

1. Why are you doing this?
2. What does it look like?
3. Who are you?
4. What is your address?

Donna thought the whole thing would be far more self-contained if they were also asked, 'If it goes off, will you promise to shut yourself up for the next fifteen years?'

* * *

From a WPC's report on a female prisoner: 'Her motions were particularly slow but she admitted she had been glue-sniffing.'

* * *

The WPC had spent four years in Liverpool. During that time she had dealt with riots, rapes, burglaries and a murder, all with the utmost calm and professionalism. But when walking down the market-place late one night with a colleague, she suddenly stopped and let out an ear-piercing scream.

'W-what is it?' asked her companion anxiously.

'There!' She pointed to an old second-hand clothes shop window. 'That dummy ... it moved!'

The PC stared deeply into the gloom of the shop – and the old chap who was rearranging his display stared straight back.

* * *

A rather sad young man in a fit of depression jumped from the fifteenth floor of a Sheffield building. His journey down, although swift, was not easy, as he lost on the way an arm and both legs to various protruding obstructions. He hit the concrete with a fearful thud and the WPC on her first day out was on the scene within seconds. There was obviously nothing that could be done for the jumper, so everyone's concern then turned to the girl.

After all, it was not the sort of situation that even the most battlehardened copper would care to find himself in. The first car raced to the scene and found the girl looking quite puzzled.

'Are you all right, miss?' asked the inspector anxiously.

The girl raised her vision from the remains and stared for a moment at the inspector. 'Eh? Oh yes, yes sir, I'm fine ... but isn't he *little*?'

* * *

Ex-WPC Mary Turner tells of an intriguing entry in an official police log book at a little sub-station at Addington. Apparently, the station was not manned at night and any officer entering the building was obliged to show in the authorised book the purpose of the visit, reason for entering and time of departure. The new young WPC made the following entry on the last line of a page; *'Entered building with Inspector Wilson for sexual intercourse'* – every subsequent reader speedily flipped the page to continue – *'allegation by young girl.'*

* * *

One afternoon WPC 37E Garrad was looking after three lost cockney kids. There were two small boys of about ten years old and a little girl of about the same age.

'Wot's the time, miss?' asked the first boy.

'Half-past two.'

'Cor, I won't arf cop it, I've missed me class!' came the worried reply.

151

'Wot school d'you go to?' asked the little girl.

'St. Josef's,' answered the lad.

'You a cafflick, then?'

'Yeah.'

'I ain't,' answered the girl proudly. 'I'm a provident.'

* * *

Ivy Robinson joined the police in 1940 during the blitz. She had but three weeks' training, which included first aid and court procedure. With little idea of what to expect, she then commenced her first stint of night duty. Ironically, that passed smoothly enough; it was after she had fallen asleep the next morning that she had her first surprise. Ivy shared a small top-floor room with another recruit and, in addition to the window and door, there was a small trap-door that led out onto the roof. A loud knock woke the girls and she was amazed to discover the superintendent, chief inspector and a large, jet-black chimney sweep, standing in the corridor.

'Sorry to wake you,' barked the superintendent, 'but we need to have access to the roof.'

Still dazed, Ivy stepped back to allow the trio entry. They had no sooner stepped out onto the roof than they were back again. Ivy's puzzled expression must have asked the question for her.

'Yes, sorry about this,' muttered the superintendent, 'but before I signed the chit, I wanted to make sure the brush had cleared the chimney-pot.'

* * *

The delightful but extremely naive WPC was always having problems with her pet cat. It always seemed to be at the vet's for one reason or another. Returning to the station after two days' leave, a colleague asked, 'How's your pussy, Janet?'

'More problems, I'm afraid.' She sighed sadly. 'I was so desperate last night that I even rubbed "Vick" on it.'

'I bet Vick enjoyed that!' enthused a passing PC.

* * *

WPC on the early-turn parade: 'When I got up at five o'clock this morning, the guy underneath me was not at all impressed.'

She rapidly clarified the situation by claiming that she had just moved into a flat.

* * *

The little old lady had been struck by a car but appeared surprisingly well.

'Now are you really sure you're okay?' asked the anxious WPC.

'Yes, my dear, I'm fine,' assured the cheery victim. 'A little wind in the shoulder perhaps, but that's all.'

* * *

WPC Helen Boddy struggled valiantly into the station with a large dog that had 'broken its leg, Sarge'.

The vet was called but the dog obviously took a dislike to him because he ran away.

The station officer rather tersely suggested that Miss Boddy be put down instead.

* * *

Sunday mornings in many parts of London are peak reporting times for thefts from cars. This is simply that many people only see their vehicles on Sunday. The actual theft may have been carried out days before.

WPC Linda Franklin had just dealt with five thefts from vehicles in just over thirty minutes, so she could be forgiven for her response to the sixth.

Worried victim: 'My car's just been stolen!'

Surprised WPC: 'What, the *whole* car?'

* * *

Brand new WPC using her personal radio for the first time in relation to an 'incident', her voice rising an octave after each sentence: 'The suspect is in Beaconsfield Road riding a motorcycle ... with no crash helmet ... no gloves ... no jacket ... and well ... Oh! ... NO NOTHING!'

* * *

Sometimes I wonder if the personal radio improves day-to-day communication quite as much as we thought it would. Take PC Paul Keyte's message to WPC Liz Madew, for example.

'Liz, can you stop that blue van travelling straight towards you?'

Liz: 'Er, do you mean that yellow car turning right?'

* * *

The young WPC filled in the criminal record description form and under 'Marks and peculiarities' inserted: *'Has the South London stutters.'*

'What's that, gel?' asked the station officer. 'Diarrhoea peculiar to the manor?'

* * *

WPC Sharon Cunningham borrowed a pencil from a male colleague. 'This is ever so warm,' she said. 'Where's it been?'

'In my deep groin pocket,' whispered the lender breathlessly.

'Ugh! I've just licked it!' grimaced the girl.

* * *

A particularly frosty-faced woman police sergeant – who was also unpopular, to boot – walked into the Reading police charge-room just as the PC was about to give the station officer the evidence for a drunk in charge of a motorcar.

'Hallo, beautiful!' beamed the prisoner cheerily. 'What's your name?'

'That's good enough evidence for me,' responded the station officer. 'He's well pissed.'

* * *

The trouble with using slang terms in everyday police conversation, is that they frequently find their way into official reports, where they appear out of place, to say the least. Take the WPC who reported an accident on a pedestrian crossing, for example: 'The zebra was correctly illuminated with a flashing light at each end.'

One up his nostril and the other ...?

* * *

WPC Bernie Walsh attended a selection board for a possible transfer to the CID. Her car, as Bernie's cars were wont to do, broke down. The embryonic detective therefore arrived fifty minutes late. After a mildly calamitous interview, she was finally asked the old chestnut of all selection boards. 'If you are lucky enough to become selected, what is your ambition?'

The girl dutifully replied with the stereotyped answer that applicants for generations have made up. 'Oh, to take promotion, of course, sir.'

'Hm,' said the chairman of the board thoughtfully. 'I thought it might be to obtain a more reliable vehicle.'

Seeking then no more than a quick and dignified exodus, Bernie swung her hand down under the chair to grope for her handbag. She missed it first time. She swung again, then again and then once more. No bag! She had left it outside with her coat.

'I didn't mind failing,' said Bernie later. 'But I did have a feeling that they thought I was a one-armed, unpunctual ape.'

This story in fact had a happy footnote – she passed!

* * *

WPC Jenny Harper was on patrol with her male colleague and tripped for the third time in fifteen minutes.

'What on earth is the matter with your feet today?' asked her puzzled male companion.

'It's not me feet,' explained the girl, 'it's me pony-tail.'

'Your pony-tail?'

'Yeah, it's too high. It pushes me hat down over me eyes and I can't see where I'm going.'

* * *

Ruth was a delightful-looking Scots WPC; her figure, hair and complexion could not have been bettered. There was, however, the slightest of 'kinks' in her nose. No one thought it detracted in any way from her looks but nevertheless the girl saved up her pennies and bought herself a nose job. The effect was stunning! In spite of the closest of scrutinies by all of her colleagues, no one was able to 'see the join'.

'But isn't it a very difficult operation?' asked her friend Josie. 'I mean, I wouldn't even know how to begin to go about it.'

'It couldn't be simpler,' explained the serene Scots lass. 'You just look in some books ... then you pick your own nose.'

* * *

Conversation overheard in a busy South London front office:

Inspector Payne: 'Dr Merchant said that the sudden death we went to the other day had Hepatitis "B", which is highly contagious and he recommends that everyone who came into contact with the body should have a jab.'

Worried woman police sergeant: 'I don't fancy that much.'

Inspector Payne: 'Don't worry, Sarge, the doctor said it'll only be a little prick.'

Worried sergeant: 'I know all about his "little prick", thank you very much. The last time I had it, it left me with an enormous bruise and a splitting headache.'

* * *

After a series of indecent assaults in a fairly localised area, it was decided to use an attractive WPC as bait. Putting on her shortest skirt, she tarted herself up and swished her hips around the area for close on three hours. She finally returned to the station with her spirit broken and her ego in tatters. The nearest she had got to an indecent assault was a wink from an elderly dustman.

* * *

It was during these assaults that WPC Alison Fry was required to obtain a written statement from each of the victims. They all more or less told the same story. Running footsteps, a glimpse of a black face, a quick hand up the skirt and a painful seizure of the victim's crotch.

At least, that is what it should have read but on each statement taken by the WPC she had used the word 'crutch'. The detective-inspector was not happy. 'These are a series of quite indecent assaults, young lady,' he said irritably. 'You've made them read like a little lad collecting catapults.'

'Now, Watch My Lips . . .'

From ex-Commander Leslie Shaw

During the street disturbances of 1981, I received a deputation of local ethnic community leaders who wished to make a formal complaint to me. My office had never looked so tidy or efficient as I prepared to meet the four-man and two-woman deputation. My sergeant announced the arrival of the group and made the first moves to usher them into my office.

I do have a rather silly habit of leaning back on the rear two legs of my desk chair and tucking my hands into my trouser side-pockets. In order to do this, my wrists loop over the chair-arms. I had managed to perform this little routine all my life without mishap – until, of course, the arrival of that deputation. Like I say, it *is* a silly habit.

My chair passed the point of no return just as the group were about to enter the room. It wavered momentarily as the first two entered, then with gathering momentum I simply disappeared from their sight beneath the desk. The first impression that party had of a police commander was of two waving feet, followed by a pause, then a head rising up from behind a desk wearing the weakest of forced smiles.

The astonishing thing was, not one person present gave the slightest indication that anything was amiss. It was as if they assumed that this was some strange constabulary routine that all police commanders undertake before receiving visitors.

* * *

Tonbridge police telephoned a Dr Richardson. 'Is a Mrs Mary Mason a patient of yours? Because she has just died.'

Dr Richardson (thoughtfully): 'Mrs Mary Mason ... Mrs Mary

Mason? D'you know, I'm not sure. Could I have a quick word with her?'

* * *

Police regulations clearly state that all prisoners must be visited hourly in their cells but, if they are drunk, then a visit should be made every thirty minutes.

It is quite obvious that the idiot who drafted that regulation has never had cause to look after a dozen snoring drunks. Even if it was *possible* to rouse them every thirty minutes it would be dangerous in the extreme. About the safest way would be to stand outside the cell doors and poke them regularly with a long pole; anything else would be suicidal. Drunks are unpredictable enough when they are fully conscious but when they have just been woken they can be positively bear-like.

In addition to the question of temperamental inebriates, there is of course the small matter of the *time* this half-hourly roll-call would take. On any average Saturday night at a busy station it would mean deploying an officer with no other function than to wake slumbering drunks. Assuming it was conceivable to find such an idiot, he would doubtless demand danger-money before he even began the task.

Drunks, therefore, are given a quick visual once-over whenever the station officer has a spare minute– and only that if they are lucky. In this way it is *possible* for each drunk to be checked twice in an hour, or on the other hand (and even more likely) probably only once a night. It was one of these 'once a night' checks that caused PC Roy Wiltshire and Sergeant Bert Oxford (not their real names, of course, and you will soon realise why) such embarrassment.

It was a little after 2am on a cold winter Sunday that Bert Oxford first enquired about the prisoners. 'Have you looked in the cells since you came on duty, Roy?'

'Leave it out, Sarge!' protested the constable. 'I've not had a minute since I started at ten!'

'Well go down there now, will you? With the sort of luck I've been having tonight you'll probably find one of them has hung his bleedin' self.'

Ten minutes later a white-faced Wiltshire returned. 'No one's actually hung themselves, Sarge, but the drunk in cell five is as dead as Queen Victoria!'

Oxford knocked over two chairs in his dash from the office. 'Oh I knew it! I bloody knew it!' he moaned repeatedly to himself. Racing down the corridor, the sergeant saw a cell door invitingly open. Inside lay a body, uninvitingly dead.

Claude Arthur Barton was not just dead – he was as stiff as a board. 'Bloody Hell!' exclaimed Oxford. 'He must have been dead for hours! I bet no bugger's looked at him since yesterday afternoon!'

'What's to do then, Sarge?'

Oxford snapped his fingers as a thought struck him. 'Quick lad, the boiler-room!'

'Sergeant?' queried the puzzled constable.

'The boiler-room,' repeated Oxford. 'Nip down there and stoke the bloody thing up. Then come back here and give me a hand with chummy.'

'Sarge, you're never going to put him in the boiler –' began the horror-stricken Wiltshire.

'Of course not, you bloody fool!' explained the sergeant. 'We'll just lay him alongside it for a while and raise the body temperature a little. That way he won't seem to have been dead for quite as long when the divisional surgeon examines him.'

An hour and a half later, Doctor John Shaftesbury, a divisional surgeon of many years' standing, finished his examination of the body in cell five. Closing his bag he walked thoughtfully back into the front office. Bert Oxford knew the chance of fooling the old surgeon was remote; he therefore raised an apprehensive glance at the doctor's entry.

'Well, he's dead right enough, Sergeant,' agreed Shaftesbury. 'And when I say "right enough" that is exactly what I mean– *right* enough.'

'Er . . . I don't think I quite understand, doctor,' mumbled the puzzled sergeant.

'Well then let me explain,' began the doctor as he sat down to write out his report. 'It would appear that the deceased in cell five is rather unique. In fact I would go as far as to say *totally* unique. You see, the left side of his body has been dead for about forty-five minutes, but the right . . .' He paused and glanced pointedly up at the old brown wall-clock. ' . . . has been dead for all of six hours.'

* * *

The harassed PC on the station switchboard had been trying to explain a particularly simple procedure to a member of the public. After the sixth attempt, he raised his eyes and exclaimed to no one in particular. 'Bloody Hell, but this woman's thick!' He then returned to the telephone and resumed his conversation.

'Look, I'll say it just once more, very slowly. Now, watch my lips...'

* * *

It was a little before noon on the 9th July that I first met Danny Wilson's right testicle. The date remains indelibly in my mind. I had entered the Gents at Carter Street police station when I saw a wincing figure standing on tiptoe alongside a washbasin. The aforementioned testicle, together with the rest of Danny's genitals, were dangling over the side of the basin and being liberally splashed with cold water.

On any previous occasion that I had observed a fellow performing strange ablutions in the men's lavatory it had been my custom to stare straight ahead and pretend I hadn't noticed. However, I couldn't very well ignore Danny – he was a great personal friend. To discover him in some distress with his manhood in his hand and his watering eyes closed in pain merited at the very least an enquiry.

'Er – problems, Dan?' I asked sympathetically.

The eyes tearfully opened and the head turned slowly in my direction. Not a word was uttered but a slow and deliberate nod of the head indicated that, if nothing else, Danny most certainly did have problems.

His head then moved once more. This time it was a brief nod down in the general direction of the washbasin. I bent forward gingerly to examine – and suddenly there it was! Yes, indeed yes, Danny unquestionably had a problem. Such a problem that it fetched tears to my own eyes in sheer sympathy.

Perhaps at this stage it may be as well to relate exactly what I already knew about the unfortunate testicle, for it certainly had a chequered history. Although this was the first occasion that I had actually laid eyes upon it, I had certainly heard a great deal about it. It was, Danny would modestly claim, at least three sizes larger than his left testicle. There was, he had told me, a valid reason for this. It stemmed apparently from being blown up in the Ardennes whilst being terribly brave against the Nazi panzers. To be fair, there was another reason put forward by his more dubious friends. Sadly it was one which Danny himself had rather indiscreetly leaked after a rather sociable evening at the local British Legion.

In this second version, the deformity, whilst still a wartime wound, had been sustained not by attacking a panzer as much as retreating from the first-floor window of an out-of-bounds Brussels brothel that was being raided by the military police. Apparently he had been about to jump from a bedroom window when he slipped and fell with legs astride the window sill. An accident that pains even the listener, never mind the victim. How then did this battle-torn part of Danny's anatomy now come to be dangling over the edge of a water-filled basin? Well, the tragedy, it appeared, had been somewhat self-inflicted. If he had but kept his mouth shut it would never have happened.

It had taken place some thirty minutes earlier in the station canteen. It was the practice of the manageress to sell off cheap, or even give away, any perishable commodity before closing for the weekend. In addition to a now curly cheese sandwich, there had been two stale doughnuts and a rather deformed bread roll. PC Brian Flynn had almost finished his morning break and was investigating anything going free at the canteen counter. Crunching hard on a stale doughnut, he asked Danny if he fancied the solitary bread roll.

'Roll!' sneered the disparaging Daniel. 'That's not a roll! My right testicle is bigger than that.' Never one to resist a challenge, Brian offered a fifty-pence bet that Danny was exaggerating. 'You're on!' exclaimed the confident Dan.

A Formica table top was cleared and half a dozen interested constables gathered round to see fair play. The roll was placed on the table; Danny took up a position alongside and unzipped his trousers. The impending gladiatorial appearance of Danny's genitals distracted attention from the contents of the dastardly Brian's hand. There was a smooth flourish by Danny and there on the table, alongside the bread roll, with its dimensions clearly superior to that of its competitor, was an abnormally large right testicle. Five fair-minded coppers nodded in unison. Credit where it's due, they agreed; the half a quid now clearly belonged to Dan.

Never one to take defeat lightly, Brian then revealed himself in his true colours. His fist, the contents of which were only fleetingly visible, crashed down towards the table. A split-second later, immediately after the first of Danny's ear-piercing screams, the results of his handiwork were there for all to see. Emblazoned across the red and now throbbing testicle were the formal words of the station-stamp: *'Carter Street Police Station. July 9th 1976.'*

* * *

Harassed Stoke station officer on a particularly busy Saturday night to a driver who has just failed the alcotest: 'These crystals have turned yellow, which indicates to me you have blood in your body.'

* * *

Station officer to the first of two prisoners in a Newcastle charge-room: 'And who is he?'
  Prisoner: 'My brother-in-law.'
  Station Officer: 'Yes, but who is he married to?'
  Prisoner: 'Oh, I don't know that.'

* * *

PC Frank Ellul was on the telephone to the loser of some tools.
  'And are you on the telephone at home, Mr O'Shaughnessy?'
  O'Shaughnessy: 'No, sur.'
  Frank: 'Well are you on the phone at work?'
  O'Shaughnessy: 'Yes, sur, but that's a secret.'
  Frank: 'Well is there a telephone number where you can be reached?'
  O'Shaughnessy: 'Yes, sur, this one, sur.'

Frank: 'And that is?'

O'Shaughnessy: '928 . . .'

Frank: 'Thank you, Mr O'Shaughnessy. So whose number is that?'

O'Shaughnessy: 'It's mine, sur.'

* * *

A well-known delusion-suffering female called at Peckham police station to casually announce, 'I've been robbed, raped and buggered.'

PC who had heard it all before: 'Oh yes, luv, and what time was that?'

Suffering female: 'How the hell do I know? He stole my watch as well.'

* * *

Senior officers are, in the main, treated with the respect required by their rank. Just occasionally, however, an instinctive lower-rank response will slip out. Take, for instance, the Newcastle superintendent who was checking his list of 'trained pistol marksmen' in the station front office. The door opened and one of the senior station constables entered.

Superintendent: 'Ah, PC Wright. Are you an authorised shot?'

PC Wright (in a rather concerned voice): 'Why, sir? Aren't you feeling well?'

* * *

From ex-Sergeant Bill Prowse

Lee Road police station in South-East London was an essential landmark for many continental visitors to these shores. Situated as it was next to a public lavatory, it proved irresistible to hundreds of foreign tourists. The mere function of 'spending a penny' would in all probability mean the tourist's first contact with the natives since

167

arriving at Dover a few hours previous. If during the course of this function problems arose, then the few yards' walk to the local nick would resolve all. Well, at least this is what they thought. After all, it is a well-known continental fact that 'all British policemen are wonderful'.

Each year, in early spring, the Lee Road coppers would watch eagerly for their first 'swallow' to arrive. This would usually be in the form of a pallid French youth with a fringe of red beard and a vast haversack. Having eased his bladder his next thought would be to ease his mind. This would mean finding out just where the hell he was. He would present himself at the police station counter with his entire English vocabulary: 'Yous 'ostel?' He would, of course, have made no prior arrangements and his problems would now happily belong to the constables. Half an hour's telephoning might possibly produce the promise of a hostel bed in Highgate. A similar period would then be needed to explain the route to the young adventurer. Lists of directions would be written down and little 'stick man' pictures of buses and underground trains drawn. The guest would then make his exit, amid a perfect frenzy of handshaking and cries of 'Bon chance!' A few minutes later, the slight figure would be seen, bowed under its mountainous haversack from which a tiny tricolour would flutter bravely. As his skinny little legs strode manfully off into the distance, we would realise he had yet one more problem. This was that on leaving the station, he had completely failed to reorientate himself. As a result, he would now be heading happily back in the direction of Dover.

As a result of these international encounters, many of the staff at Lee Road became quite linguistic. It would be commonplace to hear the most unmotivated copper conversing in fluent French, e.g. 'You've got ter allez round the corner to le bus-stop, where you will get le bus.' Or even as one 'German-speaking' sergeant helpfully directed, 'You've gotten ter gitten der bus rounden der cornen.'

Of course there was just the occasional copper who, for reasons only known to himself, would never attempt any verbal communication. He would transmit every required direction with gestures. The problem with this, of course, is that gestures are so open to misinterpretation. Long-serving Lee Roadians can still remember the two Turks who as a result of a careless wave thought they had been given permission to camp for the night. An hour later, they were still having to be forcibly restrained from pitching tent in the station yard.

An interesting belief of many visitors will soon become apparent to the newest recruit. This is that London is just a slightly enlarged version of their own home town. They simply have no conception of the size of the place. 'See you in Main Street, London, England, three weeks today!' they shout to their friends as they drive off on the first stage of their journey from Little Springs, Missouri. In this connection there was the strange case of the Swedish football team who were apparently convinced that there was only *one* motor coach in London – theirs. They had descended from it to sample the amenities of the Lee Road urinal. Emerging some five minutes later, they climbed blithely aboard a completely different coach. This one was scheduled to take a group of solid South London citizens on a two-hour tour of the hop-fields. The singularly unobservant driver at once drove off with his burly blond cargo. Two minutes later, the hop-loving party also emerged from the lavatories and were confronted by a coach of a completely different colour and a vast quantity of Swedish football gear. They were not pleased. It was almost two hours before the Nordic athletes reappeared. Apparently it was the third hop-field before the driver sensed a misunderstanding may have arisen. The Swedes then trooped into the station grinning delightedly, making friendly guttural noises and insisting on shaking hands with all present – even a drunk who had just been released.

Of all the adventurers who called at Lee Road, though, the most voluble and certainly the most emotional was a small Italian gentleman. He had a motorscooter, he had an enormous pile of luggage – and he had no wife. We were about to congratulate him on this happy state, when it emerged that he *should* have had a wife. She most certainly was on the pillion when he left Dover – now she was not. She had no money, no passport, could speak not a word of English and she almost certainly had a very bruised posterior.

The Kent police were asked to search but though the route was scoured all the way back to Dover, there was no trace of the signora. It was by then well past midnight and the unhappy husband was verging on hysteria. Torrents of Latin lamentations rang throughout the station, until at last we managed to bed him down in the belief that time is a great healer. At 4am the missing wife was located. Not bruised and battered in some Kentish ditch but safe and sound in a convent in Saffron Hill, where she had been deposited by a kindly coach-driver.

169

She had, it appeared, never been a passenger on the scooter at all. As she prepared to seat herself on the pillion it had been suddenly removed from her by the eager acceleration of her dearest – if now no longer nearest. Never had the station witnessed such demonstrations of unfettered joy and gratitude as those displayed by the delighted husband when the news was broken to him. Neither had the sergeant been kissed on both cheeks before. Well certainly not during working hours. The ecstatic Italian insisted on noting the names of all present and announced that he was a marble-mason engaged in the production of the finest headstones. To our consternation he vowed each of us would receive a sample of his best work to keep against the day of our burial. Nothing could shake his resolve and he departed, still assuring his worried audience of the rare treat that lay ahead of them.

For months after, any lorry stopping in the vicinity of the station was viewed with the utmost trepidation but providentially no tombstones ever arrived. It may have been the import restrictions that saved us but it is probably more likely that our friend's reception by his now infuriated wife may have convinced him we had done him no service whatever.

* * *

Irate woman complainant at Chesterfield police station: 'And you police don't even protect me. I could be raped in my bed while I slept and I wouldn't know a thing about it.'

* * *

Entry on a Plymouth crime sheet: *'Did steal a first aid box containing assaulted bandages.'*

* * *

Entry on a Colwyn Bay crime sheet: *'In company with his brother Graham, did severely smash the window.'*

* * *

'Marks and peculiarities' again: *'Has a thirty-two-inch scar on his left chin.'*

* * *

From ex-PC Fred Comner

Some suburban stations were at one time supplied with a maroon which would be fired from the station yard just before the Remembrance Day parade. These maroons were pointed at one end and, when preparing them for firing, the point had to go into the firing mechanism first.

In the 1970 parade at Harrow, the supplied maroon *did not* have a point – it was more of a rounded end. Someone put the thing in the wrong way up. As a result, when it was fired it came out of the mortar and shot across the yard eighteen inches above the ground, clearing it in record time.

* * *

Statement made by irate lady customer to an intrigued PC who had been called to a dispute at a Tottenham second-hand car dealer's.

'Okay, so I know my husband wasn't interested but is that any reason why I should have had to play with the thing for an hour before it showed any sign of life? It wasn't until the RAC whacked it with a hammer that I received any joy at all.'

* * *

East Ham station officer to not-the-brightest-PC-in-the-station via the personal radio: 'So how many people are there, would you say?'

Not-very-bright-PC, after a long pause: 'Approximately two.'

* * *

The two West London crime prevention officers were to give a talk to a large community association on a housing estate where muggings had become particularly prevalent. The pair of them decided on widespread publicity and drew up a small but dramatic poster with a caption in striking capitals that read – 'BEAT THE MUGGERS!' This they fed into the station photocopier. Unfortunately a few evil-minded colleagues tampered with the master sheet and several dozen posters were distributed before their attention was drawn to the new caption, 'MEAT THE BUGGERS!'

* * *

Two prisoners, one male and one female, were waiting to be charged with shoplifting in a Birkenhead police station. The female was eventually taken into the surgeon's room to be searched by a WPC. Before leaving the room, she turned to the station officer and, pointing at her accomplice, said, 'Watch my money, he's a bleedin' thief.'

* * *

Most people know about the blind love of a mother. Daughters, it would seem, are slightly more perceptive – that is, if the description by one young Portsmouth lady of her missing middle-aged father was anything to go by. Under the heading 'Marks and peculiarities' she nserted, *'Smells a lot'*.

* * *

What's in a name? One May evening in 1978 at Carter Street police station in South London, a gentleman called at the counter in some distress. 'Can you help me?' he begged. 'I'm lost.'

'Have you any idea at all where you live?' asked the station officer.

'No.'

'Do you know your name?'

'Yes – it's Basil Compass.'

Prior to his arrival that day, a coal-black West African girl named Linda Liquorish was reported missing. *After* he had left, a Mr Arthur Sillyman ost his car.

* * *

'When did you lose your ladder, sir?' asked the Willesden station officer of the distraught window cleaner.

''Alf an hour ago, when I was in 'ere reportin' that someone 'ad nicked me bike.'

* * *

Camberwell station message 10.55am of 13/11/82 reads: *'26 Valmar Road. Occupier has locked himself in the toilet whilst trying to squat.'*

* * *

The night-duty station officer handed over to his early-turn counterpart and told him that a prisoner in the cells was also wanted by the Essex police. 'I rang Essex earlier this morning but the bloke was a right wally. I couldn't get any sense at all out of him,' explained the night-duty sergeant. 'But as far as I could make out, Gray's police station doesn't open until 9am. Anyway, here's the number. I'm off to bed.'

Two minutes after 9am the early-turn sergeant duly rang the given number, which turned out be a home for the elderly. An angry and ancient voice soon cut in on the sergeant's deliberations. 'But I already know all this, you idiot! You told me once before ... when you got me out of bed at three o'clock this morning!'

* * *

Pompous Brighton witness on the telephone concerning a fatal road-accident: 'I wish to speak to you concerning the health of the deceased ...'

* * *

Female complainant at Enfield police station: 'I was walking along Hadlee Common near Cockfosters when I was confronted by a young man, completely naked except for a rubber cap on his head. He threatened to rape me unless I felt him.'

Woman police sergeant: 'Do you think you could describe him to me?'

Complainant: 'Well, he is naked, with a rubber cap on his head ... Oh yes, and he's impotent and particularly sensitive to cold hands.'

* * *

Harassed loser to PC Andy Rawlings: 'Have the police found my car yet?'

Andy: 'No.'

Loser: 'Well, will it be all right if I buy another?'

Andy (straight-faced): 'But if you've lost one, how can we possibly trust you with another?'

* * *

Criminal Record description form under 'Marks and peculiarities': *'He has a left wrist and both legs.'*

* * *

Extract from a South London police station occurrence book for 8th May, 1979:

The police were informed by Hetherington's mother that he was roaming the streets carrying a hammer and had apparently become mentally unbalanced. He was seen at his home on May 8th and was obviously suffering from severe persecution complex. He claimed that the National Front, IRA and the Anti-Nazi League were out to kill him and his mother was poisoning his food. He was wandering around his home carrying the hammer. He also imagined he was about to be evicted by his Asian landlord. Whilst awaiting the attendance of a mental welfare worker, Hetherington ran out of the house and confronted a neighbour with having improper relations with his elderly mother.

* * *

175

Extract from Hampshire PC's report on a fight between two female market-stall holders: 'I tried to separate them by putting a hand on each chest.'

Sure beat the hell out of a cross-your-heart bra!

* * *

From a Chesterfield charge book: *'He was arrested for the unlawful possession of an antique nun-cruncher.'*

* * *

One thing about being a police officer is that it becomes very difficult to be surprised at anything that one discovers whilst searching premises for suspects or property. The items that some people hoard are astonishing. However, one young lady did cause great consternation in Oldbury, as the entry in the 'Property Found' book shows: *'The finder found the rifle in the septic tank whilst she was searching for her aunt.'*

* * *

Criminal Record form: 'He is a single man aged ten.'

And again: 'Has appendicitis scar on his chin.'

What does our suspect dress like? Well, there we have a *really* helpful clue: 'Sometimes does not wear a hat.'

* * *

Fred Cumner remembers PC 'Joey' Brown very well. Although a few weeks from his thirty-year service, Joe was still a character who would pull any stroke for a laugh. He was also the proud owner of a large pair of glass 'Teddy Bear' eyes which he would slot in place at the slightest excuse.

One afternoon, hearing voices from behind the closed door of the snooker room, he popped in his staring 'eyes' and eased his head slowly around the door. ''Allo, 'allo, 'allo,' he greeted. 'Wot's a'goin' on 'ere then?' Chuckling to himself he then removed the eyes and looked up in order to receive the usual ribald appreciation of his colleagues – dead silence.

The chief superintendent, who was holding a senior officers' staff meeting, stared icily for a moment before asking, 'Just how long *is* it to your retirement, Brown?'

* * *

The Blue Lamp *from PC Bob Fletcher (with apologies to George Dixon and Aladdin)*

A few years ago we had a really smashing superintendent. Sadly, of course, no one is perfect. Our man's Achilles' heel was, of all things, the station blue lamp. He was barmy over it. All hell could be loose on the streets, pandemonium could reign in the charge-room, but as long as the blue lamp was switched on he was serene. It seemed that he felt it just wasn't a proper police station unless the blue lamp glowed. The fact that four faded photographs of Bill Sykes were exhibited on the station notice-board, two drunks slept soundly on the front office steps and an endless procession of policemen and prisoners made their way to and from the old building mattered not a toss. The only question was 'Is the lamp on?' and if not, 'Why not?'

The second person in the story is a fair-haired young sergeant who, competent to an extreme and very good to his mum, did have one small failing – that's right, he *always* forgot to switch on the blue lamp.

The third person was an evil old sergeant with jealousy in his heart.

177

He was always reminding our hero to switch on the blue lamp but only *after* the superintendent had noticed it was out. One day this villainous sergeant was returning to the station when he noticed that workmen had erected in the front garden the very thing that the whole station had been secretly longing for – a new flagpole! Such joy! What caught our villain's eye most, however, was the bulb-shaped top of the pole; it could *so* easily have been a new blue lamp. When the dastardly sergeant entered the station his heart leapt; the station officer was none other than our fair-haired hero who was good to his mum.

'See you've left the blue lamp off again,' said the villain with false benevolence. 'The new one at the top of the flag pole,' he answered to the questioning look he received.

'I didn't know we even had one. Switch it on for me, there's a pal,' said our blond hero, with misplaced trust.

But of course the switch could not be found. There were several switches on the master control panel that didn't seem to operate anything at all, so the station officer finally assumed that the bulb was defective. He dutifully reached for the 'Surveyor's book' and entered: *'July 27th, blue lamp defective.'* He then breathed a sigh of relief, thanked his betrayer warmly and returned to the front counter to deal with the small boy who had found his thirteenth stray dog of the week – little realising the repercussions that would follow such a simple entry.

Next morning, as the superintendent made his daily check on the official books, he discovered, first of all, that he now had a brand new lamp and secondly that it was already defective. This would never do. He therefore reinforced the station officer's signature with his own more weighty one.

Pangs of doubt began to grow in the bosom of the villain.

Some hours later two very imposing gentlemen with plastic clip-boards and plastic collars arrived and announced they were surveyors. They then had a series of huddled conversations, most of which seemed to consist of the word 'Hum'. But after two hours of searching, they retired from the station scene with their heads together still humming down the High Street like an octogenarian pop group. Two days later they were followed by a fairly undistinguished electrician with a seedy grey moustache and, one assumes, a different plastic clip-board. 'Can't do noffink abaht it until I've got the wirin' diagram,' he sniffed as he adjourned to the nearby Red Lion.

Now our villain really did have the wind up. Two days later two more electricians arrived. They were obviously very important because they did not have clip-boards and they looked very serious. The pair went from room to room, staring at ceilings and whispering in corners. They had the deliberation of surgeons who did not want to tell a patient they were taking his legs off. Finally they disappeared into the switchroom where they soon plunged great areas of the station into temporary darkness.

This sudden absence of light had interesting side effects. The detective inspector, who was playing snooker with one of his sergeants for a bottle of scotch, discovered five more reds on the table when the lights came on again; the superintendent's typist woke up in the dark and thought no one had called her and promptly booked three hours' overtime; and the PC who was hastily sent to switch on the emergency lighting got lost in the pitch-black basement. Eventually the two very important electricians emerged from the switchroom and issued a statement. The blue lamp at the top of the flagpole, they said, would not light up for the very good reason that it was solid wood – albeit blue. The two very important electricians told the undistinguished electrician, who promptly threatened industrial action. The surveyor's men hummed wisely and said they ' . . . hum . . . suspected something like that all the . . . hum . . . time.' The fair-haired young sergeant who was good to his mum wept profusely and the superintendent began looking for the villain, who in turn went sick with nervous exhaustion.

Meanwhile, the original blue lamp burned merrily away. Which only goes to prove that Aladdin was right: one should never change an old lamp.

* * *

A caller recently came into one South London station full of dust, cuts and grazes. His clothes were in tatters but he was not, it transpired, badly hurt.

'I shouldn't be here, really,' he announced mournfully. 'I should be dead.'

'Why is that?' asked the station officer curiously.

'Well, I thought I had committed suicide,' explained the caller. 'I drank half a bottle of whisky and turned on the gas and then I lay down with my head on a pillow in the oven ...' He broke off and shook his head sadly.

'So?' encouraged the station officer.

'I'd left the pilot light on in the water-heater and the explosion blew me out into the yard.'

* * *

PC Andy Rawlings was taking details of a stolen car and was filling in the comprehensive form 150.

Andy: 'Did you have a heated rear window, Mr Ryan?'

Mr Ryan: 'No, sur, that Oi didn't. It was just the normal one dat you wind up and down, sur.'

* * *

Hereford police carried out a routine road-check. The first driver stopped was a woman from a travelling fairground. She had no driving licence, insurance, or road tax and in addition she was a disqualified driver. When asked her occupation for the charge-sheet, she replied, 'Fortune-teller.'

* * *

Beat Crime No. 1949 for August 1981 at Carter Street police station, contained the following surprising entry: *'Allegation: Theft of jew.'*

Apparently they rolled this big stone away from the entrance ...

* * *

The doctor was called to the Tottenham police station where the prisoner, who was playing for time, complained he was suffering from epilepsy. On being examined he added, 'I also have a feeling I suffer from amnesia . . . but I can't really remember.'

*　*　*

The victim of the motor-vehicle crime must have really impressed PC Mark Jamieson. Under 'Occupation' Mark entered *'City Gent'*.

*　*　*

PCs Willmot and Balderstone had great difficulty in restraining a female mental patient. Later, in his report, PC Willmot wrote, *'I held the woman's left arm and left leg, whilst PC Balderstone held the other.'*

*　*　*

Extract from a crime report in Reading: *'The suspect was black, about 6ft. 2in. tall and very smartly dressed. He was accompanied by a Staffordshire bull terrier. The dog is dark brown with a white face, one white ear, one dark ear and two white paws. One of the witnesses believes he also drives a green Jaguar car.'*

*　*　*

Criminal Record form from Scotland Yard: *'Type of personality: Somewhat thick.'*

*　*　*

Station telephonist to an obviously irate member of the public: 'Will you please stop shouting and talk quieter? I can't hear you when you shout.'

* * *

'You can't speak to me like that!' exclaimed the same indignant telephonist to another angry caller. 'I'm not a police officer!'

* * *

PC Keith Brindley was attending a promotion board for the rank of sergeant. 'Can you make decisions easily?' he was asked.

'I think so,' replied the uncertain Keith.

* * *

At a drive-out petrol theft at the Heron service station in the Old Kent Road, eight gallons of petrol were stolen.

'Was a motor vehicle involved?' enquired the diligent police telephonist.

'No,' came back the acid reply. 'But this fellow had absolutely enormous plastic pockets ...'

* * *

Motor-vehicle crime No. 1001 entry: *'Vehicle was seen being driven away by the suspect. Name of the company was on the sides: Cleanaway Ltd.'*

* * *

The allegation of a Chelmsford theft read: *'While Mr Barnaby was rolling around in the road, having sustained a broken leg in the crash, a person unknown stole his shoes.'*

Dog Handlers and
Other Animals

It had been a rather distressing day all round for Len Bailey. Not only was he on night duty but his pet cat had died and he was patrolling Thornton Heath with his friend Alan, who appeared to be in the early stages of decomposition. Actually Len wasn't too upset about the cat, although his wife was. Alan, however, was a completely different problem. Earlier that evening he had consumed an over-large, and what subsequently turned out to be over-ripe, curry. He was now beginning to regret it. If *he* was regretting it, it was as nothing to Len's reaction – he was already threatening his colleague with the sanitary inspector. 'Don't have a go at me, please,' begged Alan. 'Just help me find the nearest lavatory and I'll die happy.'

Len considered he had enough problems of his own but what happened a few minutes later was like divine intervention. There was a large card on a notice board that read CATS FOR SALE. This was followed by a telephone number and an address. To compound his good fortune, the nearby call-box was actually working and the address was but two streets away.

'If you stop moaning for just one moment,' reproved Len, 'we can kill two birds with one stone here. I'll call on the lady who's selling the cats and you can ask to use her toilet – how's that?'

'How far is it?' asked Alan with a look of haunted desperation.

'About two miles.'

'What?!'

'No, I'm pulling your leg. It's only round the corner, we'll be there in a couple of minutes. Happy now?'

'Well as long as I can walk with short steps I suppose I'll have to be,' grumbled the now cringing Alan.

The house entrance was clearly illuminated and the bell was to hand. The lady answered the door within seconds but her ready smile vanished instantly. In the euphoria of discovering the ad, Len had omitted to say in the telephone conversation that he was a uniformed police officer. Not only that, but, although the two friends were not related in any way, they looked astonishingly similar. They were of the same build, fair haired and both wore spectacles. Mrs Wilkinson had opened the door expecting a casual cat-buyer. Instead she discovered identical twins dressed as coppers. One of whom burst dramatically into her hallway blurting out something about a lavatory, which she presumed he wanted to search. It took some minutes for Len to reassure the lady that she was not the victim of either a bizarre robbery or a grotesque wind-up. ('Grotesque' now being the operative word because of the noise, to say nothing of the aroma, now billowing from the nearby bathroom.)

Len had decided long before Alan finally emerged, still white-faced but relieved, that he was morally obliged to purchase at least one of her cats, if only to cover his embarrassment. What he was not prepared for was the cost. 'How much!' he exclaimed in disbelief, his face now almost as white as his friend's.

'Well, I know sixty pounds *seems* a lot for a cat,' said the lady defensively, 'but it *is* a genuine Burmese.'

The constable sighed. To even enter that bathroom in the next few hours was probably worth sixty pounds of anyone's money. 'Okay, I'll be around tomorrow with the money. Come on, Alan, back to work. Goodnight, Mrs Wilkinson.'

It was only when the pair were well clear of the house that Len began to attack the bowel functions of curry-eaters in general but Alan in particular. 'I wouldn't mind, but it's so unfair,' he complained bitterly. '*You* get the screaming shits and it costs *me* sixty quid!'

Nothing could now upset Alan's new-found serenity, however. 'Oh, come on, Len,' he said encouragingly. 'Look on the bright side. After all, she hasn't done all that well, has she?'

'How'd you work that out?' demanded the irate Len.

'Well, it's cost her a cat. I should think her bathroom now needs fumigating and when I dashed into the house I trod on her radio. Even-Steven I'd say, wouldn't you?'

Len studied his friend thoughtfully for a moment. 'If my missus doesn't like that cat, I think I'm going to kill you,' he said sadly.

* * *

A lady complainant at Poole police station was asked to make a written statement after being the victim of a ferocious dog. In spite of the entreaties of the constable, she insisted on writing the statement out by herself – and without advice.

'The dog growled frighteningly and bounded towards me ... I screamed with fright and fear. I must have blacked out because I remember nothing else until I woke up in bed with a policeman beside me.'

* * *

An overflowing bath in the flat of a voluptuous blonde nightclub dancer could be classified in the average copper's parlance as a 'bleedin' good call' but Mike Shadrack is not so sure ...

Late evening and water dripping into the flat beneath? Well, it's not a new problem, you know. Sometimes running taps are forgotten. Sometimes, of course, someone is seriously ill and that is why action must be quick and decisive.

The constable who was dealing with it made a quick call on his personal radio to the station officer. The front door proved to be obstinate, but soon the fire brigade attended and it was forced open. The PC made his way in. He quickly located the bathroom, opened the door and then ... closed it again. There was now no doubt in his mind that this bathroom was the place where the flood originated, but it was not the scene of some sordid domestic tragedy; it was the residence of a particularly large, colourful and angry *snake*.

Training they give you. Advice they give you. Stopping runaway horses, season for gameshooting, protected animals and birds, supervising the annual sheepdip: all these things may be dealt with in the instruction manual, but the officer could not recall the appropriate passage for large snakes in metropolitan flats. Who could assist here? Dog handlers? Mounted branch? No, perhaps not. Duty officer? Ah, the duty officer! It so happens that the inspector on duty there is one of those blokes who, while he can't saw in a straight line nor paint to a smooth finish, has a certain affinity for and love of animals. Telling a hawk from a handsaw is second nature to him. He keeps, or he's reputed to keep, ducks, frogs and toads, rabbits and cavies, stick insects and locusts, to say nothing – well, very little – of hundreds of fish. His wife, I'm told, drew the line at an alligator; as for a white rhino, the size of his surburban garden and the escalating price of hay precluded that. The fact is, he likes anything that moves (except, perhaps, the kids on Sunday morning).

By the time our duty officer arrived at the scene of battle, the constable, several members of the London Fire Brigade and a multi-coloured swapshop of local residents were all gathered in the approaches to the bathroom door. Now was the time to act with resolution, to prove this leadership business. With his hand on the bathroom door, he paused.

'I wouldn't go in there, sir,' said a fireman.

'That's all right, I rather like snakes.'

'Not this one, guv'nor; it's right up beside the door, sort of waving its head about and hissing through the keyhole.'

'It's a load of cobras,' remarked another voice.

'Charming,' said the inspector, but there was no doubt that he was now feeling a little rattled. Was the insurance paid up? Was the car in the garage? Was he wearing clean underpants?

The water was still dripping and, not unnaturally, the people from the flat below were expecting some action. They considered a mild April shower inside their home to be the unacceptable face of urban existence. The general consensus of opinion was to call for the RSPCA, who would know exactly what to do. This had just been arranged when the gorgeous, coffee-coloured young vision from the flat opposite remarked, 'In Thailand, where I come from, there are many snakes in paddy fields. They no hurt you.'

'Well, love,' said the inspector, 'will you please go in and turn off the tap before we all drown?'

'No, so sorry. Thai snakes are so very much smaller.'

Photographs adorning the walls of the hallway revealed that the blonde who occupied the flat was exotic, or, as a Scrabble expert might suggest, an erotic dancer; and the snake was an important feature of her act, if not her costume. A night owl among the onlookers provided the information that the young lady seldom returned home before 5am.

And still the water dripped softly into the flat beneath.

Eventually, curiosity got the better of one of the officers of the fire brigade. This fresh-faced young man pushed open the bathroom door at the merest fraction: no snake. The duty officer took over at once. Peering slowly around the door, he saw not one but *two* large pythons coiled serenely on the soaking floor at the foot of the pedestal basin. The enemy was no longer so terrible. With the bath full and overflowing, our intrepid hero stepped forward, picked his way gingerly between the coils and turned off the tap. He realised that a sheet had slipped from the washing line above the bath and was blocking the overflow. He leant forward to remove this. At that particular moment he noticed that the head of a very large and very unfriendly-looking Indian python was draped across the washing line, its fangs within easy striking distance of his right ear. The rest of this huge reptile's body disappeared and reappeared at regular intervals along the line of washing. Omitting to measure the exact length of the beast for his subsequent report, the inspector hastened to leave the room, tripping as he did so across the other two coiled pythons. Losing his balance, he fell headlong on both the sodden carpet and sodding snakes. Reflecting upon it later he came to the conclusion that he had probably woken them up.

Just as he reached the safety of the hallway, there arrived the man from the RSPCA, carrying – I kid you not – a forked stick. He took one quick look into the bathroom and hastily withdrew his head. 'Pythons. They seem to be okay,' he said in a relieved voice; 'I'll be off now,' and he walked backwards very quickly along the corridor towards the safety of his little blue van. 'Actually I'm the tortoise and terrapin man,' he added apologetically. So much for the expert.

Unfortunately, he hadn't shut the bathroom door properly, and about two metres of the restless python had glided across the top of it before anyone noticed. Everyone beat a hasty retreat to the outside corridor and slammed the front door shut. It wouldn't stay closed, of course, for it had been damaged when access had first been gained. With commendable efficiency, the fire brigade hammered into place some sheet metal and secured the door with two rings and a large padlock. The general relief as the key was turned gave way to surprise as loud crashes from within the flat were heard, punctuated by shouts; and then someone was thumping on the inside of the front door.

'Come, come, my good chaps, let me out. You don't expect me to stay in here indefinitely,' would be a polite paraphrase of the words from within.

'That's not a snake,' said a quick-thinking onlooker.

As soon as the door was opened the PC emerged, red in the face and slightly breathless. 'Thank's a lot, gents,' he said. 'A night in there is something I can do without.' He insisted that he had been sitting quietly in the living room beyond, writing his report.

Personally, I'm still not convinced that he hadn't been looking for some more pictures of the absent cabaret girl.

* * *

WPC 'Bernie' Walsh found a stray horse wandering around in the Old Kent Road in the early hours of the morning. Now, this is *not* a common occurrence. It was therefore decided to tether the animal in the station garage until a more civilised hour when enquiries could be made. Bernadette is quite a fusspot over animals and insisted the creature should have some straw, which as a commodity is as rare in the area as any horse. However, after a great deal of telephoning and many police miles, two bales were obtained. Bernadette then busied herself by making a bed for her newfound pet. It was whilst she was in the middle of this task that Inspector Lewis returned to the station. Although not aware of the horse, he was certainly aware that one of his WPCs was merrily tossing two bales of straw all over the corner of the garage. 'Hallo, Bern,' he greeted her. 'Staying the night?'

* * *

Patrick Cushion, a retired PC from the mounted branch, tells of an experience his policeman father had in East London in the twenties.

A panic-stricken woman rushed breathlessly into Hackney police station and screamed she had just seen a 'bleedin' great lion in the park!' The old station sergeant immediately sent for my father plus the station van-driver.

'Right, listen you two,' said the old sergeant wearily. 'I want you to nip out and catch a lion in Victoria Park. But whatever you do, don't forget the stiff gloves and dog-catching pole ... I'll be writing all bloody day otherwise.'

It was a very relieved pair of constables that discovered a large chow dog by the boating lake ...

* * *

One problem for any working-class boy who has fought his way up the police promotion ladder, is what happens when he reaches the rank of commander? If he is posted to 'A' district, for instance, with the Houses of Parliament, Buckingham Palace and Horse Guard's Parade, there is more than an even chance that he will be expected to ride a horse on one of the many state occasions. Bearing in mind that he may well be nearing fifty before he reaches such a rank, it is quite late in life to start any equestrian activities. A few quiet rides on a docile horse is obviously one way of gaining the necessary confidence but this is not always easy to achieve.

Take, for instance, what happened to a certain commander of 'A' district. It was his practice to venture out in the early hours of the morning and ride an elderly police nag in and out of the back streets of Westminster. On this particular occasion, he found himself in Lord North Street. Now the prime minister of the time was engaged in a relationship that caused him to spend as much time in Lord North Street as he did in Downing Street. One by-product of this association was that a suitable but discreet police presence had then to be maintained at the former address. One of the constables on duty that night was an attractive blonde girl with a blatant cockney voice. She stood on the corner of the street and watched in some fascination as a muffled figure sat nervously on the ancient nag. Now commanders, almost to a man, like to imagine their subordinates are familiar with every line of their face. Our commander was no exception to this rule. Even muffled up and in the dark, he assumed the young girl knew exactly who he was.

'Everything all right, miss?' he barked.

'Eh?' queried the puzzled girl, peering suspiciously back at him. 'Er, yeah, I s'pose so, yeah. Everyfink's fine.'

Not wishing to prolong, even for a minute, any time he was spending on a horse, the commander decided to ignore the girl's ignorance and return to the stables. Realising he could now kill two birds, he decided to pay a late-night surprise visit at Cannon Row police station. On these visits, the senior officer would be expected to sit at the station officer's desk and examine all the relevant books, such as charge-books, receipt-books and property books. During this time, the station officer will hover nervously about him. Now although he may not have cut *too* impressive a figure whilst on horseback in the dark, at the station desk, in a brightly lit office, he looked exactly what he was – an extremely smart, competent senior police officer. Even the pretty blonde WPC had no doubts at all as she entered the office.

'Orl correct, sir!' she acknowledged.

He grunted a reply.

The station officer then rashly decided it was an excellent opportunity to impress with his dedicated interest of exactly what had been going on in London's teeming streets. 'Everything all right out thère, Sandra?'

'Eh?' answered the girl. 'Oh yeah, everyfink's –' She suddenly broke off. 'Well that is ... I *fink* everyfink's fine. But yer see there was this really weird ole geezer on an 'orse ...'

* * *

Of course, some senior officers are so apprehensive of horses that during the Trooping of the Colour ceremony they may even need a little verbal assistance. Take for instance the novice commander who sat nervously astride one fidgeting horse that was rather obviously in need of a pee.

'Sit forward, sir,' side-mouthed a neighbouring Household Cavalry sergeant.

The commander looked worriedly about him but did not move.

'Sit *forward*, sir,' came a more insistent whisper.

Again no movement.

'*Forward*, you silly bastard! Forward!'

* * *

If a policeman is required to deal with a ferocious animal of *any* kind, from pythons to zebras, the tendency is to send for a police-dog handler. On reflection, this is not necessarily the most sensible thing to do. Just because these men are trained with police-dogs does not make them particularly magic with all other forms of animal life. Frequently they are not even very good with their own dogs.

Two huge Rottweiler guard-dogs escaped from the large house and grounds of a well-known South London villain. The animals discovered an open gate into a local school, where they proceeded to terrorise both teachers and children alike.

The first constable on the scene showed great self-preservation and sense by immediately sending for a police-dog handler. When the handler arrived, he took one look at the prowling monsters, and ran into the school and slammed the door shut.

'What are you going to do now, Officer?' panted the terrified headmistress.

'Stay here and be frightened with you, love!' replied our hero.

* * *

In fact, not only are dog handlers not at their best with Rottweilers but their treatment of old ladies can occasionally leave something to be desired. Our station dog handler, hearing a cry for help coming from a nearby house, discovered a tearful old lady who had accidentally locked herself indoors.

'Don't worry, love! I'll have the door opened in a jiffy!'

The old lady passed the key to him via her letter-box and true to his word, the door was immediately opened.

Two minutes later, a rather muted call was heard on the station bat-phone.

'Er, could you send some assistance? Me and me dog are locked in – with an old lady!'

* * *

Bewildered station telephonist to the station officer: 'I've got a bloke here who reckons he's got a partially dead dog.'

* * *

Horses, of course, all have characters of their own. No matter how long they have spent patrolling the dusty London streets, many never cease to hanker after the rural meadows where the grass is still green and lush. It was doubtless this instinct that caused Jimmy James's horse to be so unpopular with West-End costermongers, for that horse had a habit that left them hopping mad.

Jimmy, a sergeant and four other mounted constables were all returning to their stables in East London from a demonstration in Hyde Park. Their route took them across Oxford Street, where they were left waiting for some minutes for the traffic lights to change. The problem was that in those days all the traffic lights were pad-operated. They were changed solely by a vehicle, cycle, or even heavy footsteps striking the rubber strip that was situated in the road some twenty or thirty yards back from the junction. Each of the horses had avoided these pads and thus the group were stuck at the lights until a car or cyclist joined them.

The sergeant doubtless impatient to go home, told Jimmy James to hop off his horse and run back and jump on the pad. Jimmy was off his horse smoothly enough but as he ran back to the pad, the lights suddenly changed. The remainder of the group then crossed the road, except for Jimmy's horse, which was now unattended and showing its usual great interest in the imitation green grass that hung down over a costermonger's barrow. He gave it a good tug, shaking his head, pulled it clear and began to chew it enthusiastically. Unfortunately, there was about five hundredweight of fruit, nuts and best Jersey Royal potatoes piled delicately on top of it. The apples and oranges that cascaded so gaily down Oxford Street did so to yells of dismay and dire threats of cockney retribution.

* * *

From PC Andy Wilson

'Snapper' Harrington was a short, dapper and dry cockney. He was also an immaculately turned out mounted policeman who fired out words like a Gatling gun – loud, brief and straight to the point.

One day, as he was assisting the guard change at St. James's Palace, a blue-rinsed American lady saw him slip a sweet into the mouth of his horse. This gesture seemed to appeal to her and, transferring her attention from the guardsmen, she began to click merrily away with her camera at both Snapper and his steed.

'I find it really touching to see anyone in uniform show affection to their animal,' she prattled as she crouched first at one angle then another. 'I guess you must love him very much.'

'I-'ates-'im-Mam!' fired the straight-faced Snapper. 'But-it-don't-'arf-give-'im-toof-ache!'

* * *

In spite of the fact that much police recruiting publicity stresses the 'unknown' that lurks around every corner, when that corner is turned and the unknown is faced, it is not every copper who knows what to do about it. Take this incident from Rotherhithe, for example.

A PC had discovered a dead horse tied to a lamp-post. (Well, go on, ask yourself, what would *you* do?) A fair amount of dialogue understandably took place over the personal radio between the constable and the station officer.

'Is the animal "attached to a vehicle or cart"?' asked the station officer, obviously reading from General Orders as he was going along.

'No,' replied the PC.

'Well ...' murmured the sergeant as he perused further down the pages, ' ... is it "in a building or yard"?'

'No, Sarge.'

'Uh-huh. Is it "adjacent to, or in the proximity of, a veterinary premise or animal pound" as defined by the act?'

'Nope.'

'I see,' responded the sergeant thoughtfully. 'So it's just your usual common-or-garden-dead-horse-tied-to-a-lamp-post then, is it?'

* * *

Stray dogs have always been a problem at police stations, primarily because they will bark – and bark *continuously*! This, of course, can make life very difficult for local residents, as the three nuns who resided next to a South London police station pointed out.

The good sisters asked if, in kindness to the animal and fairness to the sleeping residents all around, something could be done to alleviate such a noise. The station officer was able to tell them of a new procedure adopted by the Metropolitan Police in such circumstances. Approved sedative pills were slipped into their bowl of Pedigree Chum and within a few minutes the animals would be snoring happily.

The nuns, however, were not happy with this policy. Being animal lovers, they felt this could be harmful to the dogs or even make them addicted to the drug. The sergeant explained that there was no question of the pill being harmful, and he further assured them that neither was it addictive.

Although the nuns had come on a matter of complaint, the whole dialogue had been conducted in most amiable tones. It was this attitude that doubtless prompted the sergeant to suggest that, if the good ladies objected to the dogs being given the pills, would it not be a sensible alternative for them to take the pills themselves, thereby leaving the dogs to bark all night if they so desired. In this way they would at least be sure of a good night's rest.

The goodly trio politely turned down the helpful sergeant's offer and returned smilingly to their convent. Leaving the sergeant of course, to reflect that he now had the dubious distinction of being the only member of the Metropolitan Police to advise three nuns to go on the pill.

Messing About In Boats

Thames Police

It is not generally known that the Thames Police is by far and away the oldest part of the Metropolitan Police, preceding as it does its land-based counterparts by some thirty years. However, those old river pirates of 18th-century London have, pleasure boats aside, long gone. Nowadays, the whole concept of river policing has changed. Of course there are still the occasional bodies to be fished out of the water but the large-scale theft and pressganging of drunken matelots has given way to rowdy disco-boats and drifting cabin-crusers. Some idea of the new problems facing London's river police can be gleaned by the following tale provided by the *Thames Police Association Journal*. In order to save embarrassment to those concerned, the journal has couched the story in the form of a letter from the boat's master to its owners.

Dear Sir,

It is with regret and haste that I write this letter to you; regret that such a small misunderstanding should lead to the following circumstances, and haste in order to get this report to you before you are able to form your own preconceived opinions from reports in the world press, for I am sure that they will tend to overdramatise the whole affair.

We had just picked up the pilot and the cadet had returned from changing the 'G' flag for the 'H'. As this was his first trip, he was having difficulty in rolling up the 'G' flag and I therefore proceeded to show him how this was effected. Coming to the last part, I told him to 'let go'. The lad, although willing, is none too bright, necessitating my having to repeat the order in a sharper tone.

At this moment the chief officer appeared from the chartroom. Having been plotting the vessel's progress, and thinking that it was the anchors I was referring to, he repeated the 'let go' to the third officer on the forecastle. The port anchor, having been cleared away but not walked out, was promptly let go.

The effect of letting the anchor drop from the 'pipe' whilst the vessel was proceeding at full harbour speed proved too much for the windlass brake and the entire length of the port cable was pulled out by the roots. I fear the damage to the chain locker may be expensive. The braking effect of the port anchor naturally caused the vessel to sheer in that direction, right towards the swing bridge that spans a tributary to the river up which we were proceeding.

The swing bridge operator showed great presence of mind by opening the bridge for my vessel at once, but unfortunately he did not think to halt the vehicular traffic, the result being that the bridge partly opened and deposited a Volkswagen, two cyclists and a cattle truck on the foredeck. My ship's company are at present rounding up the contents of the latter, which, from the noise, I should say are pigs. In his efforts to stop the progress of the vessel, the third officer dropped the starboard anchor – too late to be of practical use, for it fell on the swing bridge operator's control cabin.

After the port anchor was let go and the vessel started to sheer, I gave a double ring 'full astern' on the engine room telegraph and personally rang the engine room to order maximum astern revolutions. I was informed that the water temperature was 12 degrees and was asked if there was to be a film tonight. My reply would not add constructively to this report.

Up to now I have confined this report to the activities at the forward end of the vessel; down aft they were having their own problems. At the moment the port anchor was let go, the second officer was supervising the making fast of the after tug, and was lowering the ship's towing spring down onto the tug.

The sudden braking effect on the port anchor caused the tug to 'run in under' the stern of the vessel, just at the moment when the propeller was answering my double ring 'full astern'. The prompt action of the second officer in securing the inboard end of the towing spring delayed the sinking of the tug by some minutes thereby allowing the safe abandoning of the vessel.

It is strange, but at the very moment of letting go the port anchor there was a power loss ashore. The fact that we were passing over a 'cable area' at that time suggests that we may have touched something on the river bed and it is perhaps lucky that the high tension cables brought down by the foremast were not live, possibly being replaced by the underwater cable. However, owing to the shore black-out it is impossible to say where the pylon fell.

Something which never fails to amaze me is the actions and behaviour of some people during moments of minor crisis. The pilot, for instance, is at this moment huddled in the corner of my day room, alternately crooning to himself and crying, after having consumed a bottle of gin in a time worthy of inclusion in the Guinness Book of Records. The tug skipper, on the other hand, reacted violently and had to be restrained by the purser, who has him handcuffed in the ship's hospital, where he is telling me to do impossible things with my ship and person.

I enclose the names and addresses of the drivers and insurance companies of the vehicles on my foredeck, which the third officer collected after his somewhat hurried evacuation of the forecastle. These particulars will enable you to claim for the damage that they did to the railings in way of number one hatch.

I am enclosing this preliminary report now for I am finding it difficult to concentrate with the sound of police sirens and their flashing lights. It is sad to think that had the cadet realised that there is no need to fly pilot flags after dark, none of this would have happened.

Yours faithfully

MASTER

* * *

Old copper reminiscing about his days in the Thames Police: 'One of the biggest problems was the persistent suicides.'

There was this bloke who kept trying to hang himself from Tower Bridge with a rubber rope ...

* * *

From Dave Brooks, Underwater Search Unit

I remember the date very well. It was Saturday, 1st October. After all, it's not every day that an Underwater Search Unit sergeant collides with a church. Particularly on his birthday. In fact it was the rotten birthday that started the whole thing off. I had broken the early morning messroom silence with the controversial offer to buy the six members of the unit a drink to celebrate. The offer was 'controversial' because sergeants do, after all, have their image to consider. I mean if sergeants go around breaking long-established force traditions such as buying drinks for the constables, well, there is no telling what it might lead to. Some indication of this could be gleaned from their replies: 'Sure you're feeling all right, Sarge?' and 'Why don't you have a nice lie-down?' – followed by a doubting shake of the head.

'No lads,' I insisted. 'I'm determined to buy you all a drink, providing of course that we don't get lumbered with a late call. If our luck holds we'll just be able to squeeze in a pint before closing time.'

Unbeknown to my five assistants and benevolent self, this open-hearted generosity was not to take place. If we had but glanced from the window we would readily have seen why. The duty boat, call sign Thames 3, was just slipping away from Wapping pier and bound for such exotic places as Fulham power station and the eastern reaches of Chelsea Creek. It was ironically around opening time that the drama first broke. Thames 3 (curse them) had arrived off Battersea church, where they located a car sunk in the shallows by Swan Draw Dock. Cussed and incompetent as they were, they called for the Underwater Search Unit to recover it.

Back at Wapping, on receipt of the message, our unit raced to its vehicle. Their excitement was betrayed by such cries as 'Bloody Hell! Don't they know it's the sergeant's birthday?' Speeding the truck parallel to the river, I was overwhelmed by the sheer naked enthusiasm of my crew. Such phrases as 'Give it some wellie – they close at three,' spurred me on to even greater urgency. Our arrival at the dock was marked by a shouted conversation between ourselves and Thames 3.

Them: 'We've found a sunken car.'

Us: 'How on earth did you do that?'

Them: 'With the latest aid to modern marine technology.'

Us: 'And that is?'

Them: 'We prodded it with a boathook.'

Us: 'So what do you want us to do?'

Them: 'Get it out, of course. We'll come alongside that empty house-boat next to the church and pick up your team.'

Now, following orders is all right up to a point, but when all's said and done *I* am the sergeant. I thought it was about time I showed it. I noticed that one of the boat crew was hatless – that would do for starters. 'Okay, we'll join you on the house-boat – but why hasn't Wilf got his hat on? It looks sloppy.'

'He's not wearing his cap, Sarge, because he thought he might get rheumatism.'

'You don't get rheumatism from caps, man!'

'You do if they get wet.'

'And *why* is it wet?'

'Because he's five feet eleven, Sarge.'

'Eh?'

'Well, if he had been five feet eight, the boathook would have gone his head. Instead it knocked his cap off into the river.'

Thames 3 nudged its bows onto the deserted house-boat and my unit clattered on board from the shore side complete with all its equipment, whereupon a hatch in the deck crashed open and a head appeared; a long blonde head with sleep-filled eyes and what looked like two days' growth of beard. God, but she was ugly! *'Whatthebleedinhellisgoinon?'*

'Sorry,' says I. 'But we are just using your boat as a pontoon. We didn't know you were in. Er, we're the police, you know,' I added as an afterthought.

'Well, you don't look like the police to me. That one hasn't even got a cap on.'

'Yes, it's on account of his rheumatism.'

'Howzat?' queried the head.

'Never mind. Go back to bed, we'll be away in a tick and bother you no more.'

Boarding Thames 3, we anchored over the car and sent down a diver. After confirming there were no occupants, I decided to remove it from the water by pulling it up the nearby Draw Dock. Using our inflatable dinghy, I paid out the line erratically shoreward, a distance of some fifty yards. This was a shame because the line I carried was only forty-nine yards, making it necessary for me to jump the last few feet. I did this with some alacrity, causing the line to whip tight across Wilf's face. This left him with what looked perilously like a duelling scar. I eventually secured the line but was a bit worried about rowing back to Thames 3 with the tide now running strong.

'Don't worry, Sarge. Just ship your oars and go hand-over-hand along the rope.'

'Will it work?' I asked anxiously.

''Course. John Wayne did it in *Back to Bataan* and he had a tin hat and a small howitzer on his back.'

The line was eventually secured and the long slog of winding the handle and inching the car from the river began. An hour later the car was out and well up on the foreshore. We then cast around for some flotsam, to use as wheel chocks. It was about this moment that the line parted.

Due to advancing muscle fatigue, we decided to summon up the aid of a traffic patrol Landrover to tow the vehicle back up the slipway. To allow the Landrover access, I considerately decided to move our truck back alongside the church wall. The footway at this wall is very narrow, only some nine inches. Unfortunately the overhang from the church was ten inches. This fact was not seen by the idiot supervising my reverse. That is, he didn't see it until half a ton of wall cascaded down on our truck. The garage sergeant who called out to report the accident was really quite nice about it. He didn't suspend me for the accident for, as he put it, three very good reasons. One, it was my birthday. Two, I kept crying. And three – most understandably– well, who would believe that a sergeant in the Underwater Search Unit would collide with a church?

There was an interesting footnote to this pantomine. Whilst securing our gear, we were approached by a woman who said, 'My husband and I (no, it wasn't *that* woman) have been trying to eat our lunch in the pub there and watch you from the window at the same time. Unfortunately our meal is now stone cold. We were frightened to eat it in case we missed something. Thank you for the best entertainment we've seen in a very long time.'

The Area-Car

Just occasionally a really outstanding act of bravery is performed by police officers. Everyone in the force will be impressed by and proud of their deeds. But just when our heroes are thinking they can walk on water, a bucketful of ice will smack them right between the eyes.

A genuine (and very well-deserved) Commendation report was forwarded to the commissioner. However, the report that was deliberately leaked to the officers involved read just a little differently ...

COMMENDATION AWARD

To Commander 'P' Division

On Friday 26th July 1985 at 0940 an armed robbery occurred at Barclays Bank Dulwich Village SE22 when three armed men raided the bank and escaped with £10,000 in a BMW car. They were seen by a PC in a panda and followed to where they exchanged vehicles to a Renault. The PC circulated the details to surrounding units via his personal radio.

Meanwhile, the Catford r/t car (call-sign Poppa 3), crewed by PC 825P WALLIS and PC 662P GLEN, was doing its usual early-morning manoeuvre of meandering around Dulwich's manor to avoid being involved in anything dangerous on the Catford manor. Unfortunately, this day their luck ran out and they were one of the vehicles that received the message that the suspect vehicle was being followed towards Forest Hill. Acting upon this information, they turned down several side turnings in order to avoid being involved. With PC Glen giving directions they inevitably got lost but continued to head towards East Dulwich's manor, where they believed it was quiet. In their confusion, they entered Langton Rise, where one of those unfortunate coincidences that occur in everyone's lifetime happened – the suspect vehicle drove into the other end of the Rise.

PC Wallis, in his haste to turn around and escape, crashed the r/t car into the kerb, completely blocking the road. In spite of the PC's vain shouts that they were not involved and just wanted to drive away and forget about it, the three suspects decamped hurriedly from their car. Although one of the three was armed with a handgun and the other with a sawn-off shotgun, the third member was armed with an inflated rubber balloon and a stick with a white flag attached. PC Glen, having served in the Royal Marines, was conversant with the tactics for dealing with armed insurgents. Putting his training into operation, he ran off in the opposite direction and screamed for assistance from PC1099P WORRALL, who had served in the Falklands. As PC Worrall's former unit could well testify, there was no reply. (He was still at home in bed.) A young WPC then appeared on the scene and after a fierce struggle with two of the armed raiders, managed to disarm and arrest them without having to call for help from the crew of Poppa 3 r/t car. This was rather fortuitous because by this time they were hiding underneath it.

The third suspect had, by then, disappeared from view. Messrs WALLIS and GLEN, knowing that the two armed suspects had been arrested, confidently left their hideout, thinking the coast was clear. Leaping into the r/t car, they drove off at a fast speed before anyone could recognise them. Unfortunately their luck was right out. The third suspect broke cover and chased after them in an effort to give himself up. The faster they drove, the faster he ran. They were at this stage approaching 60 mph. Eventually, in Wood Vale, he overtook them and laid down in front of their car. There being insufficient room either to pass him or turn around, they stopped. The man jumped into the back of the car and demanded to be taken to a police station to give himself up. They tried to talk him out of this decision but he was adamant. Conceding defeat, they drove him to East Dulwich police station on the strict business understanding they were a minicab. He agreed and they charged him forty-five quid. Arriving at East Dulwich, they dropped him at the front door and drove away quick. Unfortunately a sharp-eyed recruit copped their number and bubbled them.

Today I spoke with them and confronted the pair with the above details. After several hours of interrogation they broke down and admitted they were the officers concerned. They explained they drove away swiftly because they did not want any publicity or thanks for something which was, after all, just a routine assignment to them.

They are officers in the true tradition of this force and should be commended in their tenacity in being able to avoid any connection with this matter. This, of course, with the exception of the sharp-eyed creep at East Dulwich, who they will see later today and reward with his just desserts.

POLICE SERGEANT 101P TREVOR POTTER

* * *

Dennis Radke from West Linn, Oregon, tells of one town-deputy who could never remain awake on night duty. After reversing into a quiet spot, he fell into his customary deep slumber. He awoke, horror of horrors, way past change-over time. Half drunk with sleep, he switched on the engine and snatched the gear selector. The splintering fence to his rear certainly caused him a momentary worry, but this was quickly forgotten as the car bubbled slowly down into the depths of the town reservoir.

Dennis recalls a second deputy who would probably have been delighted to swop the reservoir for his quiet country patch.

This eager young man had given a 'ride-along' to a lady who was, to say the very least, extremely partial to law-enforcement agencies. Now, much of the county was rural and forested so the car was parked in a particularly secluded spot. Both parties adjourned to the back seat of the patrol car for an intense and meaningful discussion. On its conclusion it was discovered both doors were latched. With no door handles on the inside and a protective metal screen between front and rear seats (it was, after all, a specially designed and secure police car) the couple were trapped. The only silver lining to this embarrassing cloud, was the radio microphone that had been draped over the screen, so the officer could at least placate his conscience by listening to police messages. 'Okay,' thought our hero. 'So I'm able to call for assistance – but what now?' The town reservoir seemed cosy by comparison.

It is times like these that a chap needs a discreet but above all *perceptive* deputy in the neighbouring county. I mean, how does one translate 'I-am-in-a-state-of-undress-and-locked-in-the-back-of-my-police-car-with-a-similarly-attired-female' into police terminology? Not easily, the lad discovered.

After many attempts, including one which caused the town radio operator to drop his coffee, help finally arrived. But not, of course, gallantry. Well, perhaps that was too much to ask. Anyway, the incident was at least kept from the hierarchy but, nudge-nudge, wink-wink, everybody else seemed to be in on it.

All in all, the lady took it rather well. Except, and understandably, she declined all future invitations to 'ride-along'.

* * *

From PC Ivan St. Pierre
While serving on 'H' division during the early seventies, I was posted as operator on area-car 'Hotel One'. The driver was a well-known 'H' district copper: one Bert 'Running-flush' Douglas.

We received a call to a suspect vehicle abandoned in the middle of Tower Bridge. On arrival, sure enough, there it was. In a prime position to destroy a chunk of our national heritage. This was in the early days of terrorist activity and the sophisticated squads that would now swing into action had yet to be formed. The quick-thinking Bert decided there was only one course of action. Traffic was stopped and the bridge-keeper persuaded to raise one half of the bridge. Three of us then began to push the car towards the yawning abyss, until, when about three feet away from the edge, our attention was drawn to a man frantically waving at us ... and carrying a can of petrol!

* * *

When policemen are together in a police car they will hardly ever discuss crime. All other subjects, ranging from football to the physical attributes of the latest WPC, will be rigorously discussed. These debates are in the main fairly safe. It is, after all, almost impossible to transmit over the r/t set accidentally. *Almost* but not quite. If the receiver *does* happen to slip and pressure *is* made on the transmit button, then snatches of conversation will suddenly be heard across half of the metropolis. Just occasionally and particularly when dialogue is taken out of context, eyebrows can certainly be raised. Take the two keen gardeners who were discussing the greenhouse that one of them was in the process of erecting.

After a few splutters and crackles, their words covered an area from Enfield to Croydon.

'I can't wait to check my erection,' said the first.

'Yes, I keep meaning to ask,' said the second. 'How long did it take you to raise it?'

'Two days,' said the first proudly.

'Is it a permanent one?'

'It certainly is now!' came the confident reply. 'I've bolted it to the floor!'

* * *

President Truman was supposed to have a sign displayed in his office that read *'The Buck Stops Here.'* That same sign could be pasted on every police area-car, because any emergency call that does not have a ready slot will be sent to the car in the guise of 'a disturbance'. This will cover anything and everything, from a triple murder to, as Dan Butson discovered, the welfare of swans.

I suppose it is really a disturbance when a swan manages to embroil himself (herself?) on a fishing line in Victoria Park boating lake. I mean, if I was a swan I would most certainly be disturbed. The problem is, of course, that swans never get themselves entangled in the six-inch shallows, oh no. It must always be in the deepest, most inaccessible part of the lake, where passers-by can see just what a pig's ear the copper is making of the rescue attempt.

The call had not started off well. There are after all *five* ponds in Victoria Park – and that doesn't include Queen Victoria's fountain or the swimming pool. Now, let some poor devil who has been struck by a bus lie bleeding for half an hour and no one seems to mind (except him of course) but a swan entangled for more than ten minutes in a fishing line will cause questions in the House. The assembled crowd of mums, toddlers and old-age pensioners were already mumbling at the delay even before Dan Butson and his colleague arrived. They were therefore not over impressed when the two officers held a lakeside meeting to discuss their next move. 'A boat! That's it, we'll use a rowing boat!' exclaimed Dan. The two constables then scrambled into a boat, as much to escape the complaints of the crowd as anything else. They each seized an oar and made to pull towards the stricken bird.

It was at this stage that they made an interesting discovery. Neither could row. Not only could they not row but neither had even been in a boat before. After several minutes of thrashing about and soaking each other, they were five yards from the shore and travelling around in ever-decreasing circles. By this time the crowd had completely forgotten the swan and were simply enjoying the coppers' discomfort. Their mirth was shared by a third member of the constabulary, who, as Dan's hat fell into the water, promptly lay down on the bank and had hysterics.

After fifteen minutes of pure pantomime, the arrival of a park keeper saved the sanity of the two constables. His opening question – 'Are you having some trouble, lads?' – did not receive the reply it warranted because of the proximity of women and children. Nevertheless, he managed to pull them in to the shore and took over the rescue. He soon recovered the bird and released it from the line. The two policemen, then safe on land, felt as relieved as if they had been rescued from the wildest part of Cape Horn. On reflection though, Dan thought it had not been a total disaster. How could it have been, when so many spectators agreed it had been their best entertainment for months?

* * *

Police Inspector Lawrie gave chase to a stolen car that eventually crashed into a stationary and unattended Volvo Estate, which was owned by the local doctor. Calling on the doctor, the inspector discovered a five-pound note blowing around the front garden. When the doctor finally answered the door he was told by the inspector, 'I have some good news and some bad news, sir. What would you prefer to hear first?'

'Eh?' queried the bleary-eyed doctor. 'Oh, the bad news I suppose. What is it?'

'Well I'm afraid some bandit has run into the back of your Volvo.'
The doctor gave a weary sigh. 'And the good news?'
'I've just found a five-pound note in your front garden.'

* * *

Peter Walton from Norwood Green was called to a 'burglary and serious assault'. On attending, he discovered a white-faced, blood-stained, half-naked man, sitting in a kitchen with a tearful wife in attendance.

'Give me a quick description of the suspect,' fired out Peter. 'There are other cars in the area and they'll do a quick search for him.'

The victim gave Peter a pained look before admitting there was no suspect.

Well, no suspect other than the cat, that is.

The victim had, it appeared, been lying awake in the bedroom whilst being sent slowly mad by a dripping tap. Unable to stand it any longer he had left his bed and taken a wrench to the valve on the water supply pipe. This was situated under the kitchen sink. In crouching to tighten the wrench, it became of interest to his cat that, although he wore pyjama-tops, he did not wear pyjama-bottoms. That part of his anatomy that swung so intriguingly in front of the animal, was suddenly pounced on and securely fastened with an abundance of claws. The pain of having cat's claws in the testicles was somewhat offset by the victim's next action. This was caused by rocketing away from the animal before completely removing his head from beneath the kitchen sink.

'I'd be careful if I were you,' said Peter, trying to make light of the situation. 'Things happen in threes, they say.'

'I know,' said the man grimly. 'And they are right. I'm going to kill the cat.'

* * *

From Alan Dawson
I had just returned from the advanced driving course at Hendon and

was aching for that very first emergency call where I could race dramatically to the scene of an incident in a bedlam of klaxons and screeching tyres. When it finally came I was the third car in line in a garage queue for petrol. I could neither go forward nor back but just seethe in frustration. Minutes later, with a full tank of four-star and both cap and jaw set at a determined angle, I had made a Le Mans-type start on the two miles' dash. My two crew members, Derek Collins and Jock Barr, were probably even happier than me that my 'initiation' call was to be finally out of my system. Yet to their credit, they gave no obvious indication.

The call was to a serious disturbance in a Camberwell café. 'Knives being used' was the ominous second line of the message. I decided to avoid the normal chaotic main-road traffic by adroit use of the side streets. The route I used took me to a junction just yards from our destination. The final street of this route – John Ruskin Street – was a fairly wide thoroughfare and quite straight. That is, it was straight until the final few yards when it curved appreciably. Parked cars, a small junction and an overhead railway bridge all helped to make this a most hazardous place for a speeding vehicle.

I had driven rigidly to the police 'system' of high-speed driving, even to the extent of giving myself a silent commentary under my breath. I was about eighty yards from the curve in the road and travelling at about 60mph, when I was compelled to make my first real decision of the journey. There, ahead of me and hogging the centre of the road at about 15mph, was an old Morris estate car, with an elderly gentleman peering studiously through the spokes of his steering wheel. Should I overtake? Yes! I went past him so fast I doubt if he realised I was there. My only problem then was that I was a little too far out in the centre of the road to speedily negotiate a right-hand bend. What was it they had taught us at driving school? 'The nearside for a right-hand bend and progressive acceleration out of it.' I had to position quickly into that nearside. The result was that in swinging the speeding car from the crown of the road into the nearside, and then to immediately tackle a right-hand bend, gave our rear wheels a 'whip effect'. Even though the road was quite dry, the rear of the car suddenly began to slide. To make the situation even more interesting, parked cars blocked the nearside and a large van was positioned on the crown of the road facing towards me, with its driver clearly indicating his desire to turn right. The width between the van and the parked cars was about nine feet. Even at that speed there was still sufficient clearance for our car. Unfortunately, with the car now beginning to broadside, we were going to need at least another seven or eight feet to avoid demolishing the six parked cars, one stationary van, area-car and crew and, quite possibly, half a brick railway arch. I decelerated and turned instinctively into the skid. Really there was little else I *could* do. A split second before the impending crash, our front wheels seemed to 'bite' and, with barely fractions to spare on either side, the car leapt tiger-like through the gap.

No sooner had we survived the hazard than we were at the café. At that precise moment I could not have left my seat if my life had depended upon it. I was like a limp rag. Derek and Jock ran from the car and soon emerged with a struggling prisoner plus knife. I transported us all back to the station where, to my astonishment, nothing was said about our miraculous escape. We had a quick cup of tea and resumed both our patrol and the customary area-car smalltalk.

I had begun to think that perhaps the pair had not been fully aware of just how close I had been to killing them. Perhaps they had assumed it was all part of being an advanced driver? Could it be that they thought I was capable of such razor-edged judgement in a high-speed skid? Such faith was touching – but surely not? Yet they had said nothing – not a word – not even a hint. Slowly my confidence ebbed back and, some five hours later, I daringly drove down John Ruskin Street again. This time however, it was a casual prowl at little more than walking pace. I thought perhaps I could show them I was capable of both extremes. We were forty yards from the railway bridge when Jock finally spoke. He leaned forward from the back of the car and whispered matter-of-factly in my left ear, 'We'll nae be doin' *that* again, will we?'

* * *

Excitable York panda driver in animated conversation with another police car whilst trying to find the location of an emergency call: 'Okay! You follow us – and we'll follow you!'

* * *

From ex-Sergeant Dan Butson

Whilst searching factory premises one dark wet night in Bow, we eventually saw a suspect on the roof. This roof was some two storeys high and almost thirty feet from floor level.

I (cleverly) remained on the ground and my operator gave chase to the suspect, who leapt the low dividing wall to the premises next door. With the operator closing fast, the villain continued to jump the low walls along the row of small factories.

Just as the PC was about to grab him, the youth cleared the final wall. There was a double drawn-out cry and both dropped straight into the canal. We had the devil's own job pulling them out but, other than being cold and wet, they were both unharmed. However, the PC lost his truncheon, for which he was later assessed seven and sixpence!

* * *

From ex-PC Alan Marshall

It was a cold wet night duty on the area-car that I first saw the leg of the dummy. It was protruding from the rubbish of a builder's skip outside the partially demolished High Street gents' outfitters. We exhumed it from its grave of broken plaster and splintered counter-tops and discovered that, other than a dent or two in the head and a couple of absent fingers, the whole thing was more or less intact. Also amongst the other treasures in the heap of debris were a pair of wellington boots and a tatty old tam-o'-shanter. We dressed the dummy in these and sat him in the back of the area-car where, unclothed and bald, he looked like an obscene version of half of the Scottish drunks I had ever seen.

We decided our discovery was a wonderful chance for revenge on the area-car crew of neighbouring 'R' division, who, on the previous evening, had been spotted pushing the remains of a burnt-out vehicle from their side of divisional boundary to ours. This had caused us to be lumbered with the investigation plus a couple of hours of paperwork. Our best moment came after midnight when half of the street lighting went off by a time switch. Using this restricted visibility, we tied a rope around his neck and hung our dummy from the branch of a tree by the side of the A21. We then concealed ourselves in the driveway of a small farmhouse opposite.

After a few minutes the whole roadway was lit up by the powerful headlights of an articulated lorry with French markings, en route to Dover. The shiny wellington boots of the dummy reflected the headlights beautifully, as did the nude backside and torso as they swayed slightly in the breeze. There was the sound of a rapid gear change, then brake-lights flashed on and off as the driver of the lorry appeared to consider his next action. Finally, with a terrible hiss of air-brakes, the vehicle stopped. A very small man emerged from the cab and walked towards the 'corpse'. Then, thinking better of it, he stopped and urinated against one of the great wheels of the lorry. Zipping up, he made the short dash back to his cab and sped away in a billowing cloud of diesel smoke.

Some minutes later we heard on our main radio set a call go out to 'R' division car: 'A21, rear of Ruxley Corner, naked body hanging from a tree. Information from passing foreign lorry driver.' The 'R' division car was soon on the scene and after the driver had poked the corpse a few times with his truncheon we heard him say, 'Bloody 'P' division!' The two of them then cut down the body and threw it into the back of their car.

The sequel came an hour or so later when we heard a main-set call go to a Thames Police launch: 'By Woolwich pier, body seen floating downstream. Appears to be wearing a tartan cap . . .'

* * *

In 1958 Stan Foskett was one of three sergeants attending a course at the Police Driving School at Hendon. One of the instructors involved in their training was notoriously tight. He would be temporarily absent when it was his turn to pay for the teas and he never, but never, had any small change. In addition, he had an incredible knowledge of every discount store in the home counties. This was no small asset when one considers that many of the training runs on these courses were precisely in that area.

Halfway through the course two nights were set aside for a couple of long dark runs over unfamiliar territory. These locations were never known by the students until they reported that evening. Preparation of the car was done under the canopy of the old hangars at Hendon airfield. There, in darkness, the students would sit in the car and check the readings of the vehicle's instruments and gauges.

From the darkness at the rear of the car, one student asked enthusiastically, 'Where are we going tonight, Sarge?'

The instructor, who was about to select a gear and move off, said, 'Stonehenge.'

After a three-second pause in which the students digested the information, the voice in the back asked, 'Why's that, Sarge – you building a rockery?'

Off Duty

In January 1985, PC George Hammond from East Dulwich was horrifically knifed as he stumbled upon a robbery. After months in an intensive-care unit, numerous replacement operations and hundreds of pints of blood, George began a slow and painful recovery. Fourteen months after the stabbing and still anything but fit, his wife Angela noticed a rather familiar card protruding from his wallet.

'George! Why on earth are you carrying a donor's card around with you? You've had just about everything replaced that you started out with.'

'You know, you're right,' agreed George. 'I'll have to amend it. They can only have my pancreas and my liver.'

* * *

Commander Ted Stow retired from the force after some thirty-five years, and literally hundreds of his colleagues, of all ranks, turned out for his retirement party. Although a fair and extremely popular man, at no time throughout his career could he ever have been accused of being a shrinking violet. This was best illustrated by one of his former aides who, in a tribute, recited the following tale.

'I dreamed recently that it was many years hence and I had died and arrived at the Pearly Gates. Seeing St Peter with a clip-board, I asked if my old friend Ted Stow had yet arrived. "No," the welcoming saint replied. "He's in the other place." I looked through the gates and there on a hill I could see a golden throne with the name TED STOW emblazoned above it. I also noticed a figure draped regally upon it. "What are you on about?" I said. "There's Ted Stow, there, now, sitting

223

on that golden throne." Peter shook his head. "No, I'm afraid it's not," he answered sadly. "That's just God ... he likes to *pretend* he's Ted Stow."'

* * *

From Anthony Sherring

There was no doubt that old Inspector Fitzalan did not like PC Reginald (Taff) Thomas. No one really knew why. Perhaps it was just the chemistry, but the fact remained that he would castigate poor Taff more than the rest of the shift put together. Taff was completely convinced that the old inspector hated him. Well if he did, then the feeling was certainly mutual. To be fair to the both of them, Taff did seem to save all his mistakes for when Fitzalan was present. When the old gentleman was sick or on holiday, Taff's police work would be flawless. But the instant that Fitz returned, Taff could be a walking disaster.

The shift, or relief as it is called, had been early turn all week and by Saturday morning Taff had received so many roastings that he was almost neurotic. Not the least of them had been for his punctuality. Taff was a notoriously heavy sleeper and would regularly join the early-turn parade with only seconds to spare, still fixing zips and buttons. Fitzalan had threatened Taff that should he miss the start of even one early-turn parade, it would give him a great deal of pleasure to send Taff back home to reparade for late turn at 2pm. This would have been bad enough at the best of times but a week of rising at 4.45am does take its toll. By the weekend it is just so easy to switch off that brass-belled alarm and fall back to sleep before the brain can engage gear. There was also an additional complication. That Saturday was the night that the clocks changed. 'Sod British Summertime!' said the hollow-eyed copper. 'It shouldn't apply to Welshmen anyway. It's a stupid English idea.' Nevertheless he was worried and when he awoke from his customary night's stupor, forty-five minutes after his alarm must have sounded, it was a case of blind panic. Without tea, shave or wash, he leaped onto his rusty old cycle and pedalled frantically the three miles to the station. It was five minutes to six as he swung into the yard. Grabbing his helmet from a coathook he practically fell down the basement steps into the parade room – the empty parade room. He was too late!

Taff cursed and raced back up the stairs and into the front office. Jock Kelly was the night-duty station officer and was obviously staying on with a late charge. 'Sorry I'm late, Sarge,' panted Taff. 'Where's Mister Fitzalan?'

Jock glanced up at the clock. 'In bed with a lapful of warm bum, I should think,' grunted the Scotsman. 'What are you doing here? You've never been early in your life.'

'I'm not early, Sarge,' explained the Welshman. 'The clocks went forward last night. In fact –' He shrugged in resignation. 'I'm a minute or two late.'

'You're *early*, you pratt,' countered the old Scot. 'Can't you do *anything* right? The clocks didn't go forward last night, they went BACK! You're not just early – you're two bloody hours early!'

Taff couldn't believe this until he had examined every wristwatch in the station. Then, finally convinced, he sat slowly down and cried.

* * *

From ex-PC Chris Stark
Big John Parker was a pre-war copper in the Gravesend Force and, like most policemen of that period, found it difficult to make ends meet. John, however, had a skill that enabled him to make a shilling or two on the side. In addition to his constabulary duties, he was also a licensed waterman with his own row-boat. He made most of his money during the thick winter fogs when visibility was too bad for the ferry to run across the mile-wide estuary between Gravesend and Tilbury.

One night, in a particularly thick pea-souper, a customer suddenly became very nervous about the crossing.

'It really is very thick, you know,' pointed out the worried man, ' ... and it's not as if you have a compass, is it?'

'Don't have a compass?' snorted the indignant John. He then rummaged around in the small locker at the stern of the boat. 'Look at this then!' he demanded. 'And it's pointing north!' He thrust the 'compass' towards the nervous passenger, who then stammered an apology and sat quite happily for the remainder of the journey.

Once the passenger had alighted, John returned his old compass – or rather a one-handed alarm clock (pointing to twelve, of course) – to its bed of old jumpers in the stern of the boat.

* * *

Detective Phil Ruskin was something of a pain as a practical joker. In the two years he had been at West Central police station, he had sent half of the personnel barmy with his fake messages and fictitious telephone calls. Retribution, when it came, was staggering.

On the Thursday evening before his Saturday wedding, he had gone out for that 'last pleasant drink with the boys'. At 3.30am he was woken by a porter at Crewe station, with an horrendous hangover, no trousers – and his left leg in plaster of Paris.

* * *

It had been the sort of day that drives a man *from* drink. Every misfortune that cold December afternoon seemed to have its origin in alcohol. I had been posted late-turn van driver and it seemed I had spent most of the evening either picking up drunks from the streets, or taking them to cleansing stations to be deloused.

I should have been off duty at 10pm but it was after eleven before I finished. I had telephoned home and apologised to my wife for being late on her birthday and requested that whatever cooked delicacy she had prepared should be postponed until half-past eleven.

'Honest, I'll be home without fail this time,' I assured her. I would like to say in mitigation that I almost made it. At 11.26pm I was three hundred yards from home and moving fast. Which over an eight-mile journey is very close indeed. But at 11.26½ pm, it suddenly went very wrong – and once more drink was the cause.

I live at the top of a small but steep hill. As I changed gear for the slope, I noticed a blood-stained figure slumped on the frost-sparkled pavement. The road was particularly icy so I continued to the top of the hill (barely a hundred yards from home!) and ran back. 'An obvious mugging victim,' I thought. Oh that it *had* been! The figure was a heavily built scruffy man in his early sixties. He appeared dazed and the blood had undoubtedly come from a now-dried wound at the back of his skull. He was in shirt-sleeves but a coat lay crumpled in the kerbside a few yards away. I bent down to speak to him and instantly discovered just why he was lying there. He was *lying* because he couldn't *stand*. He was absolutely legless. I groaned in self-pity; I was being haunted by inebriates. Well, I couldn't leave him there, although I was already beginning to wonder why. I carefully, but reluctantly, sat him up and asked him where he lived. He peered at me through an alcoholic haze for a second or two, 'Num ... num ... number ... fif ... fifty-nine.'

I looked round desperately for assistance but none was forthcoming. 'Listen,' I almost hissed, 'if I hold you, do you think we can walk there? It's only a short distance.'

He peered at me again. 'You know what you are?' he blurted and without waiting for an answer continued, 'You're a f .....g diamond.' He nodded furiously as if agreeing with himself. 'Yup that's what you are, a f .....g diamond.' I slipped my arms under his and eased him to his feet. With a much too friendly embrace he clutched me tightly and together we staggered up the remainder of the hill. I remember wondering why, if he lived at fifty-nine, I had never seen him before. But the thought skipped from my mind as the mere task of keeping him upright took all of my concentration. As we approached fifty-nine, I realised he wasn't even looking in the right direction.

'You don't live here, do you?' I suddenly snapped.

Shrugging his shoulders, he beamed a happy smile at me. 'No, I don't think I do.'

'Well, where the hell *do* you live? Don't you know?'

'Er ... Lee, I think, yeah, that's it, Lee ... I live there.'

'*Whereabouts* in Lee?'

'Fifty-nine.'

'*Whereabouts* fifty-nine, for Chrissake!'

'I don't know ... but I'll know it when I get there.'

'Lee is three miles away!'

'I'll get another cab.'

'Well, you certainly won't get one around here. Especially at this time of night.' I was beginning to wonder how I had possibly arrived in this situation and I was giving some serious thought to running away and just leaving him. 'Look, if I take you to Lee, do you think you would recognise your street?'

He nodded emphatically.'Sure of it.' He staggered back to my car and I sat him in the front passenger seat.

'Listen, don't you dare be sick in my car, understand? I'll leave the window down. Put your head out if you feel ill – got it?'

He nodded furiously. 'You know what you are –'

I cut him short. 'Oh, I know what I am all right – and if I didn't, I've just found out.'

'You're a diamond, a f .....g diamond,' he continued, ignoring me completely. ''Ere, it's just as well the law didn't find me, ennit? I'd be well nicked now, wouldn't I?' The idea seemed to tickle him and he laughed uproariously.

'Shut up and get in the car.' I was absolutely perished on the short drive to Lee. When I had left home early that afternoon, I hadn't dressed for an open-windowed midnight drive, especially at five degrees below freezing. To make matters worse, when we finally arrived in Lee, the fool still didn't know where he lived. I drove around for some twenty minutes, becoming more and more desperate in each succeeding street. I had just decided to cut my losses and dump him at Lee Road police station, when he murmured quite casually, 'I know that street.'

I slammed hard on the brakes. 'What street?'

'That one back there, the one we've just come out of.'

'Why didn't you say so when we were in it?' I demanded.

'Well,' he muttered in a hurt tone, 'I wanted to be sure.'

I did a neck-jerking three-point turn and raced back to 'that street'.

'I fink you go down here and I live over there somewhere. Fifty-nine it is.'

'You said that once before and you were bloody wrong.'

'No, no, not this time. This time I'm sure of it.' With that he gave the slightest of nods and closed his eyes.

'Don't you dare sleep!' I screamed. 'You're supposed to be looking for your house.'

'Fifty-nine it is – I just told yer,' he said through closed lids. I again braked hard. He rocked forward and opened his eyes, peering inquisitively all around. 'Are we here already?'

'How do I bloody know?'

'Er, just a minute, I think it's down there, mate.' He pointed to a narrow lane that led to a housing estate. 'Fifty-nine it is.'

'I know the bloody number,' I said through gritted teeth. 'It's engraved on my mind.' As the lane narrowed I slowed to manoeuvre around numerous parked cars. I suddenly noticed a sign: '43-81'. 'Is that your place over there?'

'You've done it, mate, you've done it! You're a f .....g diamond, you are.'

I couldn't get him out of that car quick enough. I had leapt from my seat, raced around to his side and unlocked his door before he had even unfastened his safety belt. 'Now, are you definitely sure this is where you live?'

'Of course, number fifty-nine. I told yer, didn't I?'

Having come so far, I decided to check he had the correct house, although there was no way I wanted to be alongside him when he rang that bell. When we were a few yards from his door and I was quite satisfied he lived there, I bade him a quick 'Good night'.

'Whoa, wait a minute, mate. Hold on.' With that, he thrust his hand into mine and gave me a tightly crumpled note. I pulled my hand away and the note fell to the ground. In attempting to pick it up he promptly fell over.

'I don't want your money, that's not why I fetched you home. Now *please* will you GO IN!'

'Not till you take the note. You're a dia—'

'All right! All right!' I conceded. I had already decided it would be easier to take the money than argue. Easing him to his door, I walked swiftly away. Once I was at a safe distance, I looked back and saw a hall light shining from a now opened door. He disappeared inside and the door closed.

Twenty minutes later, I was recounting to my wife just why her birthday supper was ruined for the second time. 'I just couldn't get rid of him,' I explained. In an effort to give credence to my story I remembered the pound note. I pulled the tatty, screwed-up note from my pocket. 'He wouldn't let me go until I'd taken a quid from him and —' I stopped in mid sentence. It wasn't a one-pound note, it was a *twenty*-pound note! 'Oh sod! But I can't keep it, not twenty quid, I can't. I'll take it back – but not tonight,' I added hastily. 'I'll take it back tomorrow on my way to work.'

Just after one o'clock the following afternoon, I gathered up my courage and rang the bell of number fifty-nine. A pleasant-faced but obviously harassed lady came to the door.

'I fetched a fellow back here last night,' I began.

'Was he with you?' she cut in.

'No, no! Not at all.' I then explained the previous night's happenings.

'He's very ill,' she said anxiously.

'He was very *drunk*,' I pointed out.

'But he's in hospital with a fractured skull and he can't remember a thing. I was hoping you might be able to piece things together.'

I felt awful. In my attempts to get rid of him I had forgotten all about his injury. She had apparently been able to discover that he had been for a celebration with some friends and had fallen over in the pub. They had called a taxi to take him home, but because he couldn't remember where he lived, she suspected the driver had then thrown him out. Which was doubtless when I had appeared on the scene.

'I'm very sorry, luv. I just want to return his money. He was obviously too drunk to realise.'

'You know what's bothering him most, even more than his fracture, don't you?' I shook my head. 'His teeth! He lost his teeth somewhere and as it's only a few days before Christmas he's worried sick.' Making a few more sympathetic noises I gave her the money and went on to work.

That night, as I reached the hill again, I stopped. There was nothing to lose. The teeth could just as well be there as anywhere else. And they were! A top and bottom set, smiling up at me from the gutter! I wrapped them in a handkerchief and took them home and cleaned them. The next day, wrapped in Christmas paper with a greeting card dangling, I handed them to the lady. 'Here you are, luv. A Christmas present for him.'

'Oh, he'll be over the moon! Why don't you call into the hospital and see him? Although he still can't remember anything. Otherwise, the next time you're in the market look him up. He's got the florist's next to the baker's.'

For one reason and another, it was several weeks before I actually got around to visiting the florist's. As I approached the shop, I could see an extremely smart, late-middle-aged man arranging a floral display. It suddenly struck me that I had no idea of my man's name, or even what he looked like. The only occasion I had seen him it had been quite dark and he was filthy dirty, bloodstained and toothless. Could it be possible

that this smoothie with the chysanthemums was my drunken acquain-
ance of just a few weeks ago?

He looked up and beamed. 'Yes sir, what would you like?'

'Oh, er, nothing really,' I stammered. 'I just wondered if you were the
bloke that I found without his teeth a few days before Chris ...' My
question drifted off as I realised how ludicrous it sounded.

His pleasant professional manner disappeared and his eyes narrowed
angrily. ''Ere, what's your game?' he demanded. 'Sod off!!'

I laughed nervously. 'Now it's nothing to worry about and I know it
does sound silly, but ...'

'If you don't sod off I'll ring the law!'

I raised my hand in a gesture of surrender. 'Don't worry. I'm going,
I'm going,' I assured him.

'Too bloody right you are!' he snapped. 'I want no one putting the
squeeze on me.'

I walked back to my car in total confusion. How on earth could I tell
a bloke, who can't remember, that I gave him his teeth for Christmas?
And me a f.....g diamond, too!

* * *

With many graduate entries in today's force, there can sometimes be an
element that old-time coppers would have great difficulty in coming to
terms with. The graduates themselves are usually fine – albeit a little
dim. But their wives, or sometimes their mothers, have plans for them
that certainly do not include the motley lot they work with.

Take the young sergeant's wife who decided the whole rank of
sergeant needed socially uplifting. Booking a formal dinner at a rather
exclusive out-of-town restaurant, she invited several sergeants and their
partners to what she planned to be the first of a series of intellectual
soirees.

What the poor girl had unfortunately overlooked was that the vast
majority of sergeants had not been within miles of a university. This
applied particularly to one – Peter Cage. With twelve years' naval
service before even joining the force, Peter soon began to find the
evening a drag. Misreading Peter's disinterest, the girl unwisely decided
to involve him in her current topic, which was exotic food and its taste.

'Tell me, Peter,' she asked grandly, 'have you ever had a quail in aspic?'

'No,' Peter admitted solemnly. 'But when I was in the Navy I once had piles in Singapore.'

* * *

Carter Street police station in South East London once displayed a fine garden that was a joy to see. It won numerous prizes and even received a royal visit. Sadly, old Ernie, the pre-war copper who tended it with such loving care, retired and the garden fell into neglect. This was best illustrated when the knee-high grass, that had previously been an immaculately trimmed lawn, was cut to reveal a dead cat, an assortment of fast-food cartons and a black suspender belt. Eventually the works department arrived with the sad intention to convert the old garden into a new car-park. Once the decision to scrap the garden was made, there was an undignified scramble to acquire all the bits and pieces that had accumulated in the garden over the years.

The two officers who cottoned onto this first began sorting out the contents, like tramps at a jumble sale. Eventually one of them spotted a very rare prize – a huge sack of Fisons Number 4 general fertiliser. Being something of a novice gardener himself, he consulted his partner for advice on the suitability of the product for his little back garden in Welling. Now his friend, who although having many faults could never be accused of failing to give advice, particularly on matters he knew little about, assured him that this product was undoubtedly made with little back gardens in Welling solely in mind. The intrepid gardener therefore carried his burden to that little corner of suburbia, happy in the knowledge that his blessed plot would soon be the envy of all his neighbours. Liberal amounts of the mineral were scattered to all parts of the garden and, just as if the gods had given approval, a shower occurred and washed the life-giving product into the soil.

Next morning, old greenfingers glanced out of his window and was a little surprised to discover a crust had formed over the whole garden. Being a somewhat quick-witted individual, he realised something was amiss. Also being rather courageous, he telephoned Fisons to seek their advice. 'Well,' said the Fisons man, 'can you describe the fertiliser to me?' A lengthy description followed. 'Well,' repeated the Fisons man, 'what you have most certainly isn't Fisons Number 4. That has been out of production for years.'

'What is it then?' asked our horticulturist, anxiously.

'Cement,' said the man.

* * *

Ex-PC 'Chesty' Sadler tells of the wartime day that he had an enormous stroke of luck. He was due to marry on the Saturday and, just days before, managed to hire *two* Rolls Royces for the occasion. This wartime luxury was almost unheard of and the proud, excited young constable found himself eagerly looking forward to the two 'firsts' ... his wedding *and* his ride in a Rolls!

The great day finally dawned and the groom and best man exchanged anxious glances as they waited at the church for the purring Rollses to arrive. Sure enough, exactly on time, the two silver vehicles glided elegantly around the corner with the beautiful bride and her entourage. What a sight! With all his friends and colleagues in reverent attention, Chesty's heart was fit to burst.

Thirty minutes later, the happy couple stepped out into the sunlight with the whole congregation clustered dutifully behind. The photographer disappeared beneath his cape as the group adopted their fixed, nervous wedding-picture smiles.

Suddenly Chesty's smile totally vanished. The two Rolls Royces ... they weren't there! In their place stood the station general-purpose car – and the black maria! A 'friend' had decided it would be no end of a good wheeze to switch vehicles! That customary feeling of wedding-day bliss had all but vanished from the young constable's mind, its place being taken by murder: those two cars had cost him a fortune! He looked around in total bewilderment. Everyone was laughing happily and, as for the bride's family, they were delighted. They had never ridden in a black maria before!

Of course, it is just possible that the culprit may have been forgiven – except that he also left the newlyweds a wedding gift at their flat. It was a gift that was unfortunately not discovered until several weeks after the nuptials. It was a gift that caused them to move curtains, lino, carpets and furniture. It was a gift that haunted the house by its all-prevailing presence. It was a gift that finally caused the floorboards to be lifted.

It was a large and, by the time it was discovered, fermenting carton of fresh-water mussels.

* * *

The wife of a rather rotund sergeant was in an advanced state of pregnancy and for the final few days of her condition she needed his help to dress. As he left for work, on what transpired to be the day of the birth, she put her head out of the bedroom window and called after him down the street, 'Peter! You've forgotten to put my tights on!'

* * *

By the very nature of their work, police officers do suffer some very unusual injuries, none more so than dog-handler PC Roy Squires. Limping into the station one evening, he was rather reluctant to explain the cause. It turned out to be a somewhat painful off-duty branding. Whilst preparing to leave for work, Roy had sat quietly meditating in his darkened lavatory. The unlocked door suddenly swung open and his wife, with a baby in one hand and a teapot in the other, tipped three scalding teabags into his very exposed lap – then, chattering cheerfully to the baby, closed the door behind her.

* * *

From Patrick Cushion , ex-Mounted Branch
Bill Weston, apart from being a mounted policeman, was a friendly, affable sort of fellow who really enjoyed his food. If he wasn't actually eating it, then he was most probably talking about it. So when Jock Salmon, a stable companion, mentioned he was off back to Scotland for a holiday, Bill soon steered the conversation around to haggis. It had

een one of Bill's lifelong regrets that he had never even tasted the stuff. He had heard talk about it, of course, not all of it favourable, but never morsel had passed his lips.

'I'll tell you what, Jock, you send me one while you're away and I'll ay you for it when you come back – okay?' Jock readily agreed.

Now there were two problems with this conversation, the first being that Jock forgot the haggis just as soon as he left the station, and the second that the entire dialogue was overheard by the remainder of the mounted staff. A few days later, a visit to the local butcher's secured a sheep's stomach, and a variety of rather disgusting ingredients, mainly consisting of horse feed, was inserted. The result was packed carefully into a box, a few second-hand stamps plastered neatly on the corner and postmark smudged. After a brief explanation to the station officer, that gentleman rang through to the stables to tell Bill that his eagerly awaited parcel had arrived.

It was with great excitement that, later that day, Bill unpacked his haggis' onto the kitchen table. It was then that he experienced his first difficulty. This was that in spite of an assortment of cookery books, he didn't have a clue how to cook it. Unsure how long a haggis stays edible, Bill decided against waiting for Jock Salmon's return. Instead he approached a neighbour who had spent all her formative years north of the border. Of course there is no logical reason why any Scot, male or female, should be proficient in the culinary art of haggis cooking. It would doubtless have been easier if the lady had admitted as much. Keeping a safe distance from the creation, Bill's advisor recommended a good long boiling in a large receptacle'. Having then done her neighbourly bit, she hastened back to the sanctuary of her own premises.

The faint aroma of the uncooked haggis, although a little strange, was not particularly offensive, which was more than could be said for once it was cooked. The 'faint aroma' became a rather strong smell, that in turn became a stench and evolved quickly into a taste – a bitter taste that crawled up Bill's nostrils and lay on the back of his throat like quinine. The Scottish advisor was quickly summoned once more and pronounced an expert opinion. 'It's off,' she said briefly. 'And if I was you I'd bury it.'

This was distressing news indeed for the affable William. After all, his old pal had interrupted his holiday to send the thing to London. Still, there was no doubt that something was wrong with it. It would be three more days before the dustmen called; by that time it would have taken over the street. His neighbour was right, he must bury it.

It was another ten days before Jock returned from his leave. Not wishing to embarrass his friend, Bill made no mention of the health of the haggis, except to thank him profusely for sending it. 'It was delicious,' Bill lied. 'Perhaps a little strong – but yes, I quite liked it.'

Jock found this gratitude, to someone who hadn't even sent a postcard, very strange indeed ...

* * *

On the night the Leman Street police station closed its doors for the last time, there was a party to celebrate the passing of this monument to Victorian architecture. This was held in the adjoining Garrick pub.

The guest of honour for the evening was Mr Jack Wolkind, the Town Clerk, who arrived sporting a neat black bowler hat. It was the custom of the then chief superintendent, Mr John Thornton, also to sport a bowler. As the magic hour approached, a few wags decided that the chief superintendent's hat would look better for a little reshaping. These 'alterations' were done by the delicate use of a few size twelve duty boots. It was only when the Town Clerk came to leave that it was realised that the adjustments had been made to the wrong hat. Still, he took it well. A quick whip round and a grovelling apology alleviated any sense of grievance.

* * *

The beautiful but blatant cockney WPC was excitedly looking forward to her holiday tour of California.

'Where do you go first?' asked a male colleague with only mild interest.

''Eef-Row,' answered the girl, proudly.

* * *

236

he two PCs were discussing their outside interests during a recent
ND demonstration.

'My classes finish this week,' said the first.

'I haven't been to mine for a while,' said the second. 'I wonder if they
ave also finished?'

'What are you studying?'

'Car maintenance – but my car broke down and I couldn't go any
ore.'

* * *

he metropolitan police are, by and large, an unceremonious lot.
nlike the forces of many capital cities, where special days are marked
y festivities, the force now has no real ceremonial side at all. Even the
eremonial tunics have long been withdrawn. One of the few times
ormality is shown is to commemorate a state occasion or a VIP death.
n such cases the station flag will flutter, either at the top, or halfway
own the flagpole. It is safe to say, therefore, that weeks, even months,
an go by without the flag seeing the light of day.

It was this assumption that caused half a dozen coppers from Carter
treet police station in South London to 'borrow' the thing for their
oliday in the Greek Islands. The group had hired a boat for a couple
f weeks and thought that the old blue flag would look very impressive
even if the crew looked a mess. In theory, it was an idea that should
ave worked well; they could have eased it back into the locker on their
eturn without anyone even missing it. In practice, they had two strokes
f bad luck. Firstly, the flag was stolen as soon as they landed and
econdly, and even more unkindly, someone shot the Egyptian
resident.

Now, chief superintendents who have crimes on their manor of ten to
welve thousand a year, are understandably touchy when someone
inches their flag; it must somehow seem like the last straw. By the same
oken, the six coppers who lost it were not over-happy, particularly
hen they saw it fluttering on the roof of a quayside taverna. Eventually
commandos-style night raid was launched and the flag retrieved.

237

Meanwhile, fifteen hundred miles away, there was hell to pay. A dead president and no flag! Cupboards that had not been disturbed since the days of Robert Peel, were being turned out by the score. All manner of treasures came to light – but no flag.

That night, the raiding party understandably celebrated their success – a little too much, as it turned out, because when they awoke the following morning the flag had disappeared again. The gallant crew decided that on their return home they would keep their heads down and say nothing about the disappearing ensign.

They had been back but a week when a mysterious parcel was delivered to one of them at the station counter. It contained, of course, the flag. There was no explanation or note of any description, there was simply the flag. In the absence of a better idea, the recipient slipped it into the appropriate locker. This coincided with the chief superintendent ordering one last great search of the building. As a result, the old flag now flies as proudly as ever ... on high days and funerals.

*   *   *

During the 1950s and early 1960s, the pay of the lower ranks of the force was so low that most married men 'moonlighted' purely in order to manage. This practice was greatly frowned upon by the police establishment and was classified as a serious breach of discipline regulations. Many men were dismissed from the service for such action and therefore it was vital that great discretion and secrecy were used.

The test of discretion was never greater than that faced by the early turn crew of one South London police car. A call had been received to go to a local cemetery, where a grave-digger had sustained a heart attack and fallen into the grave that he had just completed digging – two hours after finishing night-duty on the same police car!

Courts

The Old Bailey court had recessed for lunch midway through the evidence of PC Malcolm Burridge, who was the second of two police witnesses in a serious assault trial. On the resumption, the defence counsel broke from his original line of questioning by asking the constable, 'Were you not told, Officer, not to discuss this case during the lunch-break?'

'Yes, sir.'

'And did you not speak to PC Richard Flynn, the previous witness, in the court canteen?'

'No, sir! He spoke to me.'

'Who spoke to whom is irrelevant, surely!' snapped counsel. 'The point is that you were expressly forbidden to converse. What was the nature of this discourse?'

The policeman shuffled uncomfortably and looked towards the judge for help. None was forthcoming – in fact his lordship then added his own weight to the questioning. 'What did the previous witness say to you, Officer?'

'Er, well my lord,' stammered Malcolm, 'PC Flynn said ...' Once more he swallowed nervously. 'Er ...' he said, '"The way the defence counsel is performing, we're home and dry."'

* * *

WPC Bernadette Walsh, who has legs up to her shoulder-blades, sat in the back of the Crown Court listening intently to the case in which she had just given evidence. Her attention was suddenly drawn by a tap on her shoulder. She turned to see that her friend and colleague, PC Ian Hill, who was sitting two rows behind, was mouthing a silent message.

241

The girl could not make head or tail of this conversation and so eased herself from the seat and leaned towards the whisperer. All would have been well except that the hinged seat slowly tipped, without Bernadette realising. The attempt to resume her position resulted in an almighty jumble of arms and legs as she slipped headfirst backwards to the floor.

The clatter caused his lordship to look up from his deliberations, just in time to see Miss Walsh's thighs waving around in the air. To compound the disturbance, Ian Hill, who had so valiantly tried to restrain his laughter, promptly broke down in gales of hysterical cackling which stopped the trial immediately. His lordship, finally taking his eyes from the thighs, asked the cause of this disturbance.

The clerk of the court, who, perhaps for some biological reasons, seemed immune to the inverted maiden's limbs, announced in extremely bored tones, 'The young lady has fallen from her seat, m'lud – and the officer is laughing.'

'A very worthwhile interruption,' enthused his lordship as order was restored.

* * *

Chairman of the bench at a Juvenile Court passing sentence on a 'misunderstood' fifteen-year-old: 'I see you have fourteen previous convictions. If you are not careful, Anthony, you will become a criminal.'

* * *

The probation officer was interviewing a young prisoner at Chelmsford court and asked, 'Do you live with your parents?'

'No,' replied the youth. 'My father was killed a few weeks ago in a plane crash.'

'Oh, I'm sorry to hear that. Was it one that we heard about?'

The prisoner shook his head. 'No, it was in the West Indies.'

'Not the Bermuda Triangle?'

'No,' said the puzzled prisoner. 'Engine failure.'

* * *

Warrant Office
Sutton Magistrates Court
Shotfield
Wallington
Surrey
9.9.86

Dear Mr Cole,

I produce a short story from the old Wallington Warrant Office, which you may consider suitable for your book.

The small magistrates court in Wallington, Surrey, jogs my memory and takes me back to one morning in the spring of '83, when the whole warrant office staff of five were assembled. Heads were down, and silence reigned, as work on diaries, register and cash books took place. One member of staff, a civilian Clerical Officer, whom I shall call 'Auntie', was in the process of collating police papers for the Summons list of the morning. 'Auntie' was a very efficient, lovely lady, whose knowledge of police, and particularly court, routines was of the highest order. However, as we were all suddenly to learn, her vocabulary in certain directions was far from extensive. Reading through an officer's process book, and the statements it contained, she suddenly broke the silence. 'Bollocks – that's a funny word.' Heads of all male officers were raised in unison, as smiles, chuckles and one amazing belly laugh filled the air. No one present could bring themselves to explain.

JOHN CROWE
POLICE SERGEANT

* * *

Graffiti in the dock at Willesden court: *'Do not ask for bail as refusal often offends.'*

* * *

Many magistrates are known for the acidity of their humour. In response to the regular defendant's request of 'Can I have time to pay, sir?' one Lambeth magistrate would usually reply, 'Certainly. You have ten minutes before the prison van arrives.'

* * *

A rather smooth detective was giving evidence in Hendon court *re* possession of drugs. 'The prisoner was found in possession of a brown herbal substance, your Worship. It is currently being examined by the Metropolitan Police Friendly Society –'
Magistrate: 'Er, perhaps "Forensic", Officer?'

* * *

Ex-Sergeant Dennis Traher recounts one dialogue he heard in court. The prisoner had been remanded on bail and had failed to appear.
Constable: 'I'm sorry, Your Worship, but the defendant has excreted.'
Magistrate: 'I'm sure he has, Officer, but don't you mean "estreated"?'

* * *

In cases where the defendant has little or no defence, it is common court practice for defence counsel to attack the credibility of police evidence. This will usually take the form of identification, such as the position of the witness in relation to the offence, the distance he was away, and so on. One particularly insistent counsel at Snaresbrook crown court stuck in Dennis Traher's memory.

Counsel: 'You claim, Officer, that you could clearly see the car number-plate from where you were standing?'

Constable: 'Yes, sir.'

Counsel (somewhat desperately): 'You must have particularly good eyesight, Officer.'

Constable (perhaps a little too proudly): 'Yes, sir, I have.'

Counsel (perking up at the slight hint of a mistake): 'Oh you have? Perhaps you'd be good enough to recount to the court the most distant object you could identify that night?'

Constable (realising the trap in the very nick of time): 'Well it was a very clear night, sir, and I had absolutely no difficulty in seeing the moon.'

* * *

Sometimes members of the public just do not see the law in the same serious way that the legislature intended.

PC Mark Blenkinsop stopped a motor-cyclist who had no lights on his machine.

'Where is your rear-light assembly?' asked the inquiring Mark.

'The elastic band broke and it fell off,' explained the surprised rider.

* * *

The charge sheet for a certain Miss O'Leary made interesting reading. *'Occupation: Lesbian.'*

* * *

Anyone who believes that we all speak the same language has obviously never spent very much time in a court of law. There, one common function can be instrumental in provoking two different vocabularies.

Take Frankie Grant, for example. Frank was appearing for stealing a motor-car. He was a dear little lad of sixteen. He had obviously made a serious attempt to impress the court with his appearance. His tight jeans, loose boots and off-white stained vest were more than matched by his multifarious tattoos, shaven head and solitary earring – in his nose. Frank had been arrested with a nineteen-year-old friend. Therefore he appeared in the first instance at a magistrates court and not at the far less formal juvenile court. The magistrates will always insist in such cases that the boy's parent or guardian is in court to represent his best interests.

When the case was called, the older boy stood in the dock and Frank was directed to stand in front of it.

'In this case,' said the arresting officer, 'the younger boy is only sixteen years of age, Your Worship. His father is in court.'

However, in spite of that announcement and the repeating of his name, Frankie's dad appeared quite reluctant to step forward.

'Frank,' beamed the smiling titled lady magistrate. 'Where is your father?'

Frank stopped picking his nose and sniffed. 'He's gorn for a shit.'

'Er, oh I see, he has, er, gone to the loo, has he?' stammered the titled lady.

'Nah,' differed Frank. 'He's definitely gorn for a shit.'

* * *

From Cliff Morgan
Following a late-night disco in Newbridge, Gwent, a number of young men were arrested for being drunk and disorderly. One of them insisted

that his occupation be shown as 'Professional idiot'. It was therefore duly entered on the charge-sheet.

Next morning in court, everyone pleaded guilty and, as the offences and locations had all been identical, so were the fines – five pounds each. That is, with one exception.

'I see you are a professional idiot,' said the magistrate as he studied the charge-sheet closely. 'Well, as you are a "professional" perhaps you had better pay ten pounds.'

* * *

A few years ago, the now closed Llanhilleth magistrates court was held each week in the reception rooms of a local public house. Immediately outside the courtroom window was the main railway line that served the Ebbw Vale steelworks. Whenever a train passed – and these were very frequent, very slow, and very long – the whole proceedings would come to a halt without any instructions being given. For several minutes the court would find itself in suspended animation. The PC reciting his evidence, the clerk giving his advice, and the magistrate delivering his verdict – all would freeze into quiescent silence until the squealing, clunking wagons had passed.

* * *

At Brynmawr magistrates court, the defendant had pleaded guilty to a theft charge and his antecedents were being read to the court, including a very long list of previous convictions. The clerk then asked him if he had anything to say before sentence.

'Yes, it isn't fair,' protested the sulking prisoner. 'You've only read out the times I was found guilty. How about the time I got off with that burglary charge at Blaina? Then there was those taking-and-driving-aways that got slung out at Abertillery and those ...'

* * *

There are times when it seems to many police officers that the pages of the *Guardian* consist of nothing but complaints against the force. That paper, in common with many others, it is fair to say, complained strongly about the civil rights of prisoners on remand during the prison officers' work-to-rule. As a result of this work-to-rule, many prisoners who were on remand were kept overnight and at weekends in police stations and magistrates courts instead of the remand centre at Brixton prison.

The cells in these places were not constructed for such long incarcerations and hardships were almost unavoidable. Policemen were almost as fed-up with the dispute as the prisoners. However, some officers, it seemed, did put themselves out, as the following letter shows.

The Officer-in-charge
Camberwell Police Station

Cell 20
Camberwell Magistrates Court
Camberwell SE5

Dear Sir,

I feel I must write to congratulate you and your staff on being awarded a Five Star rating in the 1982 Egon Ronay Good Nick Guide.

Seriously, my experience of police and prison custody spans only the last two or three weeks, but during that time I have managed to inspect the accommodation (and sample the service) at Cannon Row, Vine Street, Bow Street, Lambeth Sorting Point, Chelmsford, Brixton and here. During the three or four weeks prior to that, I have stayed at the Hilton, the Dorchester, the Inn on the Park and several other London hotels. THIS PLACE WINS HANDS DOWN!!!!! Let me explain.

I have been conned at the Hilton, had a mouldy scone at the Dorchester, waited six hours for my breakfast to be cleared away at the Inn on the Park. Been threatened with a 'smashing up' at Cannon Row. Been refused a cup of tea at Chelmsford – when I wasn't even a prisoner. Had to wait days for sweets, stamps etc. at Brixton and been punched in the mouth by a prisoner at Bow Street, where for good measure, I also had my trousers set alight in a cell with ten people! And a few weeks ago, I was so heavily drugged by the doctors at a mental hospital that I fell out of bed and cut my eye. I agree, I can hardly believe it myself, but every word is true and witnessed.

But HERE: Friendly officers. Good food. No waiting for it. Newspapers free and without asking. Sugar in tea. Requests answered at once instead of ignored for 1½ hours. And, to top it all, someone went to the local shop and bought provisions we needed!

I still think I'm dreaming!!

Many thanks.

Best wishes,
Yours,

TIMOTHY HILLS

* * *

PC Peter Lewis arrested a particularly devious character for theft. Although well known to the police and with a host of previous convictions, the prisoner always denied guilt, usually claiming mistaken identity.

'You see,' said the prosecuting counsel rather smugly. 'The officer says he not only knows you very well but that you were the only person in the street at the time. In addition, of course, there is also the small matter of him actually seeing you steal it. Now, do you still claim it wasn't you?'

'Yes, sir,' answered Delroy. 'It definitely wasn't me.'

'If it wasn't *you*,' said counsel irritably, 'then who do you claim it was?'

'It was my brother, sir. It always is him and I keep getting the blame.'

'This brother of yours,' pursued counsel. 'Does he look like you?'

'Oh yes, sir!' exclaimed Delroy emphatically. 'We are always being taken for twins.'

'But you're not?'

'No, sir. He's older than me.'

'I see,' said counsel thoughtfully. 'How much older?'

'Three months, sir.'

* * *

Ex PC 'Chesty' Sadler remembers being in a North London court before the war when a case of begging appeared before the magistrate.

The 'beggar' was in fact a con-man who was particularly well known to the local police and made a very good living from the generosity of others. The magistrate always wore his spectacles on the end of his nose and was nick-named 'Will Hay' after the old music-hall and film comedian whom he greatly resembled. 'Will Hay' was a kindly man, who always made a point of leaning over backwards in order to be fair to those who appeared before him.

'You see, Officer,' said Will, 'the prisoner claims that he was not *begging* at all but giving a service.'

'It didn't look like that to me, Your Worship,' said the doubting constable.

'He claims he was playing "Danny Boy" on his one-string fiddle,' persisted Will. 'And as such, passers-by were simply rewarding him for his efforts. Could that be true do you think, Officer?' added the magistrate hopefully.

'I doubt it very much, sir, I really do,' said the policeman, shaking his head.

Will gave a long sad sigh. 'Very well. But why are you so sure the prisoner was not giving a service?'

'There weren't no string on his fiddle, sir.'

* * *

The defendant had pleaded not guilty to a summons for having no insurance and the PC was asking the Camberwell magistrate for an adjournment to enable a second police witness to attend.

Magistrate to defendant: 'Will you be calling any witnesses, Mr Okolaja?'

Defendant: 'God is my only witness, sir.'

Magistrate: 'Well, He's not usually available to give evidence.

Officer, how many witnesses will you be calling and what are the brief facts?'

PC: 'I'll only be calling one police witness, Your Worship. The brief facts are that we saw the defendant in the Old Kent Road pick up several people in his car. We then stopped him two miles away in Peckham and his insurance does not cover him for Hire or Reward.'

Defendant (cutting in sharply): 'I just parked and went away from my car. When I came back all those people were sitting in it and ordered me to take them to Dulwich.'

Magistrate (thoughtfully): 'Yes, Mr Okolaja. I think perhaps you may have to call your witness, after all.'

* * *

From ex-Sergeant Chris Archer
On duty as a sergeant one day, I arrested and took to the station a man for being 'drunk and disorderly'. The station officer then said to the prisoner, 'What's your occupation, mate?'

'Bloody well find out!' came back the unhelpful reply.

The station officer, who was something of a character, wrote down 'Water-diviner' on the charge-sheet.

Next morning at court the prisoner pleaded guily. The chairman of the bench, after perusing the charge sheet, remarked, 'I see you are a water-diviner. Perhaps you'd better stick to water in future.'

'Yes, sir,' answered the bewildered prisoner.

I don't think he even knew what a water-diviner was!

* * *

Sergeant Ian Whittaker to a prisoner: 'Do you have any dates you wished to avoid for bail, Mr O'Reilly?'

Mr O'Reilly: 'Yes, sur, Monday to Friday, sur.'

Sergeant W: 'No, I mean any holiday or such like?'

Prisoner: 'No, sur.'

Sergeant W: '7th September then?'

251

Prisoner: 'No, sur.'

Sergeant W (surprised): 'Why not?'

Prisoner: 'I'm on holiday then, sur.'

Sergeant W: 'Thursday 15th September then?'

Prisoner: 'What day of the week would that be, sur?'

* * *

Whenever a drunk is arrested, a 'pro forma' stating the brief facts is completed by the arresting officer. This is done purely to save the court's time. If the drunk pleads guilty, then the officer is not requested to attend court; the pro forma is read out in lieu. The 'brief facts' from one young officer stiffly read as follows:

'As a result of a complaint by a female at the police station counter, I entered the police station waiting room. There I saw the defendant urinating against a radiator.

'I said to him, "Why are you urinating against that police station radiator?"

'He replied, "Because I can't open the police station window."'

* * *

PC Douglas Cable in full constabulary flow in the Camberwell court witness box: 'The defendant is an habitual snu-gliffer, Your Worship.'

* * *

PC in Carlisle court, having reported a motorist for defective windscreen wipers: 'On examination, Your Worship, I found no liquid could be excreted onto the windscreen.'

* * *

Vital witness at the Old Bailey: 'The nearer I got to him, the further away he was.'

* * *

Prostitute witness at Inner London Crown Court, giving evidence for the defence in a case of brothel-keeping: 'Everything I did, I did off my own back.'

* * *

A bemused drunk was asked by the magistrate at Clerkenwell court if he had anything to say before sentence. 'Yes, Your Worship,' he muttered, as he looked down, shaking his head. 'Whose trousers have I got on?'

* * *

PC Fred Davis was at Camberwell court when his colleague PC Mark Haddon approached, resplendent in a new raincoat and carrying a smart document case.

'Hello,' said Fred cheerily. 'What are you doing here today?'

'Oh, I'm just looking after "Dumper" Highley's case for him.'

'Is it "griefy"?' asked the job-oriented Fred.

'Er, no,' said the puzzled Mark. 'It's brown with two combination locks.'

* * *

From a Wolverhampton dangerous-driving case: 'He drove an articulate lorry in an erotic manner.'

* * *

In the compilation of this book, I have realised there are a handful of police court stories that are little more than myth, folk-lore, legend – call them what you will. They have been sent, or handed to me by serving and retired officers of all ranks and both sexes from all parts of the country. Each provider had one thing in common. None of them actually claimed to have been in court when the incident happened. Yet all of them claimed to have learnt it from a most reliable source, usually a best friend who was in court that day. I list here three of these tales. I do not say I do not *believe* them – it is possible that each story has its origins somewhere in police antiquity. I just say that there are dozens of coppers up and down the country who will *swear* to their validity.

The first of these tales concerns an elderly magistrate who is rather deaf and is hearing a case of unlawful possession of a quantity of antiques. The prisoner – as all antique dealers tend to do – denies everything, even though the entire hoard was found in the back of his shop. He claims staunchly throughout the case that the whole thing is a frame-up and he has never so much as laid eyes on any part of the haul before. The prosecution fires several innocuous questions at the dealer and then changes tack dramatically by asking, 'Just how many of these articles were in your possession?'

The prisoner then becomes thoroughly irate and begins to lose his composure. 'Fuck all!' he snaps. 'Absolutely fuck all!'

The magistrate leans forward to his clerk and whispers, 'What did he say?'

The clerk recites the prisoner's reply verbatim, "Fuck all! Absolutely fuck all!"'

The magistrate then leans back in his chair and, tapping his fingertips lightly together, says thoughtfully and almost to himself, 'That's funny, I could have sworn I saw his lips move.'

*

The second tale concerns a case of speeding in the days before the use of electronic aids. A passing car would be timed with a stop-watch over a measured furlong and, on the basis of the time recorded, the exact speed would be calculated. These speed traps were always held on notoriously fast stretches of road that would be as well known to the magistrate as they were to the police. On the day in question, however, there was a relief magistrate and, after the PC had given his evidence, the new magistrate wished to know a little more about the geography of the scene.

'Were conditions clear, Officer?'

'Yes, Your Worship.'

'Was there any doubt at all that the road was a restricted one?'

'None at all, Your Worship.'

'I see,' murmured the magistrate, taking copious notes. 'And was it on the level?'

'Oh, on my life, sir,' emphasised the constable. 'It is as true as I'm standing here.'

The final tale is usually situated in a pre-war court and invariably concerns an Indian defendant. It is discovered just after the case has commenced that there is no interpreter present. This causes some consternation until an old copper, with a veritable chestful of medal ribbons, stands up and has a quick word with the court inspector.

'Your Worship,' announces the inspector. 'This officer has spent a great deal of time in the Indian army and if it pleases Your Worship he feels that he will be able to converse with the prisoner.'

The magistrate and clerk then go into a prolonged huddle and decide that, subject to the PC being suitable, the case may proceed.

'Are you sure this man can understand you, officer, and likewise, you be understood by him?' asks the worried clerk.

'No doubt at all, sir,' says the old constable confidently.

'Very well,' agrees the magistrate. 'But you will first need to take the oath.'

The PC holds up the Bible in his right hand and recites the oath. Then, approaching the puzzled prisoner, he stares him straight in the eye and prods himself in the chest with his huge left forefinger. 'Me ... policeman ... shinee ... buttons ... You –'

'Thank you, Officer!' cut in the clerk. 'I think we will adjourn the case.'

Fontana Non-fiction

Fontana is a leading paperback publisher of non-fiction. Below are some recent titles.

- ☐ POLICEMAN'S BALL Harry Cole £3.99
- ☐ POLICEMAN'S LOT Harry Cole £2.99
- ☐ POLICEMAN'S GAZETTE Harry Cole £2.99
- ☐ POLICEMAN'S PATCH Harry Cole £3.99
- ☐ POLICEMAN'S PROGRESS Harry Cole £3.99
- ☐ POLICEMAN'S STORY Harry Cole £2.99

You can buy Fontana paperbacks at your local bookshop or newsagent, or you can order them from Fontana, Cash Sales Department, Box 29, Douglas, Isle of Man.

Please send a cheque, postal or money order (not currency) worth the price plus 24p per book for postage (maximum postage required is £3.00 for orders within the UK).

NAME (Block letters)_____

ADDRESS_____

_____